the fabulous
SKINNIE MINNIE
RECIPE BOOK

by Frances Hunter

published by Hunter Ministries Publishing Company
1600 Townhurst
Houston, Texas 77043

Canadian Office
Hunter Ministries Publishing Company of Canada
P.O. Box 30222, Station B
Calgary, Alberta, Canada T2M 4P1

Scripture quotations are taken from:

The Authorized King James Version (KJV)
The Living Bible, Paraphrased. © 1971 by Tyndale House
Publishers, Wheaton, Illinois. All references not specified
are from The Living Bible.

ISBN 0-917726-05-7

LORD, I PRAY FOR ME!

Father, thank you for the food you provide, and the many different varieties.

Thank you for the wonder of each fresh peach, each apple, each grapefruit, each orange, each strawberry!

Thank you for the beauty of lettuce, tomatoes, cucumbers, green peppers, radishes and onions. Thank you for their crispness and their satisfying flavor.

Thank you for chicken and fish, dear Lord, and for the goodness they contain.

Thank you for keeping me this day from eating the things I shouldn't eat, and thank you for teaching me to love the things I should eat.

Thank you for the reminder of the Holy Spirit THIS DAY when I am tempted to eat what I should not.

I give you the praise, Father, for what you're doing for me today!

Charles ♥♥ Frances Hunter

TABLE OF CONTENTS

ADD SPICE TO YOUR LIFE

The Christian life is fun!
Cooking is fun!
Being married is fun!
Losing weight is fun!
Keeping it off is fun!
It all depends upon your attitude.

Charles and I have had the most fabulous time trying recipes, inventing new ones, and throwing some out after we tried them! We discovered exciting new ways to prepare some of the most mundane of foods, and experimented to find foods that could be used for all members of a family by adding or subtracting somewhere along the line.

On some of the recipes we have carefully shown you how to make and serve the recipe both ways, but for the most part we're leaving it up to you and your imagination. Ask God to let you be creative where recipes are concerned, and see what he will do for you.

We've put a calorie counter in the back of the book to help you out, and I'm praying you'll get to know what to put in YOUR food, and what to leave out.

This can be one of the most exciting times of your life, if you will depend on God to take you over the rough places. "I am always thinking of the Lord; and because he is so near, I never need to stumble or to fall." Psalms 16:8

David might not have been talking about losing weight when he said that, but it's a tremendous scripture for those who feel tempted by the devil to eat a "thou shalt not."

The devil tries to make us think occasionally when we're on a food retraining program that we are weak and don't have strength to continue. Just quote this scripture to him and see what happens: "He fills me with strength and protects me wherever I go." Psalms 18:32

You get out of life what you put into it, so if you put a bad attitude into it about being overweight and unable to lose or keep the weight off, remember that's what you're going to get back.

If you go into it with the knowledge that you are a winner because of Jesus Christ, and look forward to the exciting things he'll teach you, it can be one of the most exciting times of your life.

Charles was talking to a woman recently and she said she had read the "Fat" book, but it hadn't done her any good. He asked her if she had done what the book said to do.

She said, "No."

He said, "Do you do what the Bible says?"

She said, "Yes."

He said, "It wouldn't do you any good to read it if you didn't follow the instructions, would it?"

She got the point!

And the same thing is true of you. If you'll pray that little prayer every day, it's amazing how God will let you love the things that you ought to eat.

There are two different kinds of spices you will need to make this book and your life exciting. The most important ones are the spiritual spices which you need to keep your Christian experience fresh and new. To keep that part of your life in tune with your new cooking opportunities, we've put a little "Food for Thought" after each recipe, which is designed to keep you on top spiritually.

I never knew how exciting the Christian life was until I tried it! You'll never know how exciting different spices can be until you've tried them.

To spice up your food, you might try adding a dietetic peach or pear half to your dinner by sprinkling a little cinnamon or nutmeg on either and then putting under the broiler for a minute or two until warm.

Sometimes I put a can of peaches and a can of pears together, add some cloves and stick cinnamon, warm and serve as an accompaniment to fish or chicken. If it's not sweet enough for you, add a little liquid sweetener or an envelope of the powdered sweetener.

Around 50 calories per peach or pear half, but a delightful addition to any meal.

Remember that you can always add a little ginger, lemon peel, cloves, cinnamon, nutmeg, peppermint or almond flavoring to a lot of things and come up with a whole new world of food!

Add a little scripture memorizing to your daily diet, and come up with a whole new world of ammunition to fight the devil when he tells you to eat something you shouldn't!

Add a little witnessing if you want to put some real "ginger" into your Christian life. I guarantee you it will add zest!

I'm not a doctor, nor am I a dietician, so if you have a health problem, I'd appreciate it if you would go to your doctor before you start any complete food retraining program, but I am sharing with you some of the ideas I have learned from what God has done in my life concerning weight.

I've learned that many times I'd rather have a little bit of something super-special than a whole lot of something that's only mediocre, and you may feel the same way. I've also discovered that many fabulous dishes contain very few calories.

The milkshake on the cover is one of our extra special delights, and it's only 82 calories for two!

If a recipe doesn't quite satisfy you on the first trial, add a little more seasoning, or sweetener. Remember that all of us have individual taste buds, and it's the spice you put in that makes it pleasing to you.

To make it exciting for your family, add extra ingredients such as cream, butter, cheese to give them more flavor and body.

Sin starts with an attitude, and problems with food can start with an attitude. You can say, "I don't like to eat that kind of food," or you can say, "Thank you, Jesus, for teaching me to like things I never dreamed I would like."

Most people think I diet all the time — they're wrong, I don't have to. Since giving my appetite to God, I eat what I want to, but I don't eat what I used to. He has taken away my desire for the surplus foods I ate before, which I discovered I don't need. I eat normally at meal-times, but am still on the two-meals-a-day schedule the Lord put us on when we went on our Daniel Fast.

Here are a few hints which can really help you enjoy all the little goodies in this book.

Eat enough so you won't nibble between meals.

An apple a day keeps the fat away.

It's fun being a "Skinnie Minnie."

I can have any dessert I want, no matter how rich, or how gooey, or how many calories it contains. ONE BITE!

It looks better on the plate than it does on me!

Don't wail on the scale if you cheat when you eat!

Jesus, how little can I get by with?

God thinks about me constantly!

God hears me when I talk to him about my problems!

I can personally choose to be a "fattie" or a "skinnie."

I am fat because I eat too much!

I have given my appetite to God!

I love strawberries!

I love lettuce!

I love green beans!

I love grapefruit!

I'm full of Jesus, so I'm satisfied!

Hallelujah!

MEAT, BARBECUE, SEAFOOD, CHICKEN AND TURKEY

FOOD FOR THOUGHT: "For the kingdom of God is not meat and drink; but righteousness, and peace, and joy in the Holy Ghost." Romans 14:17 (KJV).

MEAT

Where do you start, and where do you stop when you start talking about meat dishes.

Did we forget about steak? No, because that's one of the staples in the world's eating plan. We want to remind you, however, that even the hardest worker doesn't need more than four ounces per meal. Anything beyond that is excess! It may seem like a little in the beginning, but remember it's all you need!

How about roasts? Are they forbidden fruit? No, but most of us know how to cook roasts, and for the person who's looking for the skinnie minnie inside of their fat exterior, I'd suggest no more than three ounces of sliced roast at any sitting. Take your scale to the table and measure it so that you don't eat too much. Be sure to ignore the gravy, too! But if you insist on gravy, try one of the new "diet" gravy mixes on the market. They're super and only 22 calories for 1/4 cup of gravy.

FOOD FOR THOUGHT: Let's be extravagant Christians — we're extravagant with our time, we're extravagant with our money, we're extravagant with our food — that's why we are all too fat. Let's be extravagant with God — and not care what he does with us.

VEAL CUTLET CASSEROLE

326 calories per serving   Serves 1

1 veal cutlet 3-oz. size
1 can bean sprouts or use fresh
1/2 cup tomato sauce
2 teaspoons grated cheese
garlic salt, onion salt, celery salt
and salt and pepper to taste

Put all ingredients in casserole and bake 350° 30 min.

FOOD FOR THOUGHT: Love knows no bounds and is the most powerful word in the Bible except God and Christ Jesus.

VEAL SCALOPPINE WITH LEMON

247 calories per serving   Serves 6 4-oz. each

1-1/4 pounds veal scallops cut very thin (then pound
  to flatten). Cook quickly on Teflon pan or
  Pam-sprayed pan until browned.
Add 3/4 cup beef bouillon
1 tablespoon lemon juice
6 thin lemon slices
salt and pepper to taste

Simmer about five minutes. Remove meat to serving platter and top with lemon slices. Sprinkle with tarragon or parsley.

FOOD FOR THOUGHT: A mechanical Christian is a carnal Christian.

BEEF AND RICE STUFFED PEPPERS

168 calories per serving   Serves 6

Brown 1/2 pound lean ground beef with 1/2 teaspoon
  salt and pepper.
Mix with 2 cups cooked long-grain white rice.
Fill six green bell peppers with mixture.
Place in baking dish with hot water in bottom of pan.
Bake 350° until peppers are tender.

FOOD FOR THOUGHT: Fun is the counterfeit of joy. Joy en-
compasses all of what we call fun, and abundantly more. Fun is
temporary — joy is permanent.

MEAT LOAF BURGERS

266 calories per serving   Makes 4 patties

1 pound lean ground beef
2 eggs
1 onion chopped
2 tablespoons dietetic catsup
2 tablespoons skim milk
2 tablespoons sweet pickles chopped
1/2 teaspoon dry mustard
1/2 teaspoon salt

   Gently mix all ingredients together. Form into patties
and broil three inches from flame in broiler pan six or
seven minutes on each side.

FOOD FOR THOUGHT: Hold your mind open like a cup to re-
ceive instructions from God. Some people turn their cups upside
down.

HERBED MEAT LOAF

250 calories per serving   Serves 6

1-1/2 pounds lean ground round
1/2 cup skim milk
1 egg, slightly beaten
3/4 cup chopped onion
1 clove garlic, minced
3/4 cup finely chopped parsley
1/2 teaspoon basil
1/2 teaspoon oregano
1/2 teaspoon paprika
1 teaspoon salt
1/2 teaspoon pepper

Combine all ingredients; work with hands to make certain well mixed. Pack into loaf pan. Bake 350° 1 hr.

Note: This is excellent also sliced thin cold and served with a good tangy mustard, sour pickles and raw vegetables or a salad. Try a thin slice wrapped between lettuce leaves for a "sandwich."

FOOD FOR THOUGHT: . . ."But as for me and my house, we will serve the Lord." Joshua 24:15 (KJV)

SWEET AND SOUR MEATBALLS

295 calories per 4-oz. serving   Serves 4 generously

1 pound lean ground beef
1 tablespoon prepared mustard
1/2 cup dehydrated onion flakes
2 cups tomato juice
1/4 cup vinegar
1/4 cup soy sauce
1/4 teaspoon garlic powder
sweetener to equal 1/4 cup sugar
4 slices dietetic pineapple in 4 tablespoons juice

Combine beef, mustard, onion flakes. Mix well. Shape into balls and bake 350° 15 minutes or until done (or can broil).

Combine tomato juice, vinegar, soy sauce, garlic powder, sweetener, pineapple and juice. Bring to a boil and add meatballs. Simmer for four minutes. Simmering the meatballs longer improves the flavor.

FOOD FOR THOUGHT: God helps those who help those who can't help themselves.

SAUTÉED CALVES' LIVER

160 calories per serving

Allow 1/4 pound of calves' liver per person, cut in thin slices. Saute quickly in a Teflon skillet or Pam-sprayed pan until brown and crisp, but tender-pink inside. Season with salt and pepper. Top with a dab of diet margarine and a sprinkling of chopped fresh parsley.

FOOD FOR THOUGHT: God talks all the time. What have you heard recently?

BEAN CHOW MEIN

Approximately 185 calories per serving   Serves 6-8

1 pound lean ground beef
1 med. onion, chopped
1 4-oz. can mushrooms or fresh
2 cups French-style green beans
2 cups bean sprouts canned or fresh
2 cups tomato juice
2 cups water
2 teaspoons imitation butter-flavored salt
1 tablespoon chopped parsley
2 beef bouillon cubes
2 packets artificial sweetener
 (or liquid sweetener to equal 2 teaspoons sugar)
Variations: Add chopped celery, green pepper and/or carrots

Cook beef until browned. Add onions and mushrooms and cook until tender. Add remaining ingredients and simmer slowly (about 30 minutes).

FOOD FOR THOUGHT: "My words are plain and clear to anyone with half a mind — if it is only open!" Proverbs 8:9

GRILLED LAMB CHOPS

236 calories per serving

1 4-oz. lean rib lamb chop. Broil to desired doneness in preheated broiler about 2 or 3 inches from heat, turning once. Lamb chops are at their best with a nice brown crust and medium-rare inside. For chops 1-1/2 inches thick, this should take about 8 to 10 minutes. Season to taste.

FOOD FOR THOUGHT: Listen to God, not doctrine or pride.

GREENS WITH BEEF

152 calories per serving   Serves 4

1-1/2 lbs. spinach (or other greens such as Swiss chard)

Separate greens and cut into pieces. Let stand in cold water until ready to use; then drain well.

Heat 1 tablespoon salad oil and add 1/2 pound flank steak or top round steak, cut 1-inch thick, then cut in strips 1/8-inch wide and cook until beef strips are browned.

Sprinkle with 1/2 teaspoon salt and 2 teaspoons soy sauce. Stir, remove meat.

Add another tablespoon of oil to pan; add well-drained greens, stir and cook for about 3 minutes, or until greens are tender-crisp. Add 1 cup diet chicken broth. Stir 1 tablespoon cornstarch with 1/4 cup water until slightly thickened. Stir into pan with meat again. Quickly mix altogether and then serve at once.

FOOD FOR THOUGHT: Each of us lives in our own little world — win it!

BAKED SAUERKRAUT & BEEF

168 calories per serving   Serves 6

Brown 1 pound lean ground beef

Mix in: 1 can sauerkraut
                  1/4 teaspoon parsley
                  1 green pepper chopped
                  celery powder
                  2 cups tomato juice
                  mushrooms

Bake 350° 1-1/2 hours; or can be simmered on top of stove.

FOOD FOR THOUGHT: God doesn't only have POWER — HE IS Power!

CABBAGE-BEEF CASSEROLE
169 calories per serving   Serves 6

1 small head cabbage
1 pound lean ground beef
1 small onion chopped
1/2 cup uncooked rice
1 can condensed tomato soup with 1 can water

Chop cabbage and place in greased baking dish.
Brown meat and onions. Stir in rice. Pour over cabbage. Mix soup and water. Pour over entire casserole. Bake 350° for one hour. Add more water if needed.

FOOD FOR THOUGHT: Thank you, Jesus, for using me as your battleground with Satan!

SLIM LIVING SHEPHERD PIE
130 calories per serving   Serves 4

Broil 6 oz. ground beef
Add 1 cup water.
1 small can chopped mushrooms
Add 4 oz. carrots and onions sliced
Salt and pepper to taste
Simmer 30 minutes

Cook 1 pkg. frozen cauliflower until barely tender. Put in blender with liquid. Add 2 tablespoons dry non-fat milk. Blend until just mashed a little. Spray dish with Pam. Put beef mixture in, top with cauliflower. Bake 30 minutes 400°.

FOOD FOR THOUGHT: Accept all God has and BE all he wants.

BLESSED BARBECUE

Barbecues are family fun!

Everybody gets into the act, and can have what they want with no problems to the chef.

We love to barbecue, and we love barbecue in any form. Years ago I soaked the meat and chicken in so much barbecue sauce that it was impossible to tell whether it was chicken, ribs or hamburger. Then I met Charles! And he showed me a different way to barbecue, and I've never gone back to the old way.

Try this and see if you don't think it's the most succulent and juicy chicken and ribs you have ever eaten!

ribs	All your family
chicken	can eat!
beef brisket (lean)	That's all —
salt and pepper	no sauce needed.

Charles uses a barbecue grill that has a tight lid with dampers. He soaks about four hardwood chips in water while he is preparing the charcoal fire. When the flame has heated the coals to a glow, he adds the soaked wood and closes the lids, with dampers open, until the flame is extinguished, but the coals are hot. While the fire is heating the coals, he prepares the meat.

He cuts the chicken into pieces that are easy to handle. For ribs, we leave about three or four together when cooking. The brisket usually is about two inches thick so it will cook through easily.

The only seasoning we put on barbecue is salt and loads of pepper. Charles presses cracked pepper into the meat or chicken.

Your charcoal will not be white, but it is perfect and hot about the time you've fixed the meat and chicken. Put the meat on and get ready for a treat.

Charles turns the meat or chicken every five minutes until done, usually about thirty-five minutes. Remember, the secret is to have a lid on the barbecue grill so the flames will go out and the smoke will blend with the heat. Do not overcook!

Don't depend entirely on the looks, because it may not brown as much as you are used to, but it is thoroughly and deliciously done. Most barbecue is overcooked, and dry as a result.

The whole family will want to be close when the barbecue is being turned, because it smells so good! Have the table set and serve with a delightful salad as soon as it comes off the fire.

The calories aren't bad. A chicken breast (don't eat the skin) is only 115. Six ribs 1" x 4", only 245. Three ounces lean beef brisket, 115. You can double up and eat two portions of either brisket or chicken and really have a "blessed" barbecue.

FOOD FOR THOUGHT: Put a smile in your food!

GRILLED VEGETABLES IN PACKETS

90 calories per serving   Serves 4

2 chicken bouillon cubes
2 tablespoons water
3 tablespoons margarine (diet)
1/2 teaspoon accent
1/4 teaspoon pepper
4 med. zucchini sliced
2 med. tomatoes cut in eighths
1 onion chopped
1 green pepper chopped

Dissolve bouillon cubes in water over heat. Stir in margarine until melted. Add other ingredients and seasonings. Spoon mixture into six 12-inch squares of heavy-duty aluminum foil. Wrap securely. Place on grill over med. hot coals and cook 20 to 25 min. turn frequently.

Could be baked in oven also.

FOOD FOR THOUGHT: Discipline is the thread that weaves a boy into a man.

SEAFOOD

SHRIMP ORIENTAL
(or Beef, Pork or Chicken)

	Calories
1 can tiny canned shrimp	110
1/2 cup fresh mushrooms	10
1 tablespoon soy sauce	19
2 stalks celery	10
1/2 onion	20
1/2 can bean sprouts	17

Put soy sauce in small skillet and stir fry celery, then onions and last of all the fresh mushrooms. Add bean sprouts and canned shrimp. Be sure to wash the shrimp extremely well so that none of the "fishy" taste is left. Use fresh shrimp if possible.

Use 1/4 teaspoon arrowroot and thicken juice.

FOR YOUR FAMILY members who don't have to watch their weight!

Add 1 cup canned sweet and sour sauce and at the last minute, add 1 cup either peanuts or cashew nuts. Really delightful! Heat through. Serve on rice.

On top of either version, put three or four thin slices of green pepper for color, and one or two cherry tomatoes cut in half.

Serve with additional soy sauce to taste.

For a little unusual flavor, grind up a little fresh ginger.

Oriental dishes are quick to fix, because they require very little cooking. I use a wok in my kitchen and find it extremely helpful. Don't overcook anything. Two or three minutes is enough. To be efficient in cooking oriental dishes, have all your vegetables prepared in advance.

To change to beef, pork or chicken, put 1/4 cup oil in bottom of wok. Cut beef, pork or boneless chicken into 1/4" strips and drop into bottom of wok and stir fry for about 1 minute. Take out and then complete the same way as the shrimp. The chicken is especially good with the cashews. The nuts are a real "no, no" for you, however,

FOOD FOR THOUGHT: Giving ALL is not giving up all!

BOILED SPICED SHRIMP

130 calories   28 medium shrimp

Take fresh shrimp and boil with pickling spices for approximately 2-3 minutes.

Serve hot or cold. Let guests peel the shrimp right at the table, either hot or cold. Delicious either way.

I don't know what I would have done without shrimp when I was trying to lose weight, because this little sea creature packs a lot of protein and is super low in calories. I like boiled spiced shrimp served with lemon juice and soy sauce.

Charles enjoys the shrimp, hot or cold, with red sauce, made of catsup and horseradish.

There'll be no oceans in heaven, so eat plenty of shrimp down here!

FOOD FOR THOUGHT: I'm as much a nobody as anybody Jesus has available!

FILET OF FLOUNDER IN FOIL

Approximately 30 calories per serving   Serves 1

Allow 1/4 pound of filet of flounder per person.

For each portion, tear off enough aluminum foil to wrap each filet.

Lightly spread the foil with diet margarine and place fish on it.

Sprinkle with salt and pepper and, if you like, chopped parsley, a pinch of dried thyme, grated Parmesan cheese, and/or grated onion. Wrap foil around the fish, tightly seal. Put on baking sheet and bake in preheated oven 400° about 15 to 20 minutes. Test for doneness — open one of the packets and see if fish flakes easily. Serve right in the foil packets with lemon or lime wedges.

Other fish may be used (try putting a little grated grapefruit peel, and a pinch of nutmeg for an unusual taste treat).

FOOD FOR THOUGHT: "O Lord, you have examined my heart and know everything about me." Psalms 139:1.

BROILED SEAFOOD CAKES

265 calories per serving

1 small 3 oz. can salmon
1-1/2 tablespoons chopped parsley
salt & pepper
2 tablespoons dry non-fat milk
1 egg slightly beaten
1/2 oz. cheese crumbled

Combine all ingredients except milk powder and form into patties. Coat with milk powder and broil until brown.

FOOD FOR THOUGHT: You can never get honest with God until you are honest with yourself.

CURRIED SHRIMP OR CRAB

74 calories per serving   Serves 1

2 tablespoons French dressing   1/2 teaspoon curry
1/4 teaspoon liquid sweetener   powder
3-1/2 oz. shrimp or crab

Heat dressing and seasonings (add small amount of water if necessary). Toss with hot cooked shrimp or crab and serve on bed of cooked bean sprouts.

Can be served chilled also on bed of lettuce.

FOOD FOR THOUGHT: God always has miracles in process. The devil has messes in progress.

SALMON CASSEROLE

327 calories per serving   Serves 4 generously

1 16-oz. can salmon
1/2 cup frozen fresh peas cooked
4 slices extra-thin bread, toasted and grated
1 beaten egg
2 tablespoons minced onion
2 tablespoons chopped parsley
2 tablespoons lemon juice
1/4 teaspoon salt
1/4 teaspoon pepper
1/4 cup water

Remove skin and bones from the salmon, but do not drain. Mix salmon and liquid together with the remaining ingredients. Place in a greased casserole. Bake 350° for 45 min. to 1 hr. (If you do not use extra-thin bread, you must increase the calories accordingly.)

FOOD FOR THOUGHT: It's not how you fall, but how you get up that counts.

FISH TERIYAKI

224 calories per serving   Serves 6

1 cup soy sauce
1/4 cup sugar
1/4 cup salad oil
2 teaspoons grated fresh ginger root
1 clove garlic, chopped (optional)
2 to 3 pounds fish filets
1 tablespoon sesame seed
Shredded lettuce (optional)

Combine soy sauce, sugar, oil, ginger and garlic. Let filets stand in this mixture for several hours.

Line a shallow baking pan with aluminum foil.

Lift filets from soy sauce mixture and arrange in pan. Broil 5 to 7 inches from heat for about 4 minutes. Brush with a little oil. Turn, brush with more oil if necessary (just a little). Sprinkle with sesame seed. Broil 3 to 5 minutes longer, or until fish flakes. Serve on shredded lettuce (if you like). (figure 1 lb. flounder = 118 calories)

FOOD FOR THOUGHT: "He fills me with strength and protects me wherever I go." Psalms 18:32. This means when I walk through the cafeteria line, he protects me from taking the things I shouldn't eat!

TUNA SAGE DRESSING

429 calories entire recipe   Serves 2 generously

2 slices bread broken in pieces
6 oz. drained or water pack tuna
1 teaspoon sage
1/2 cup boiling water
2 chicken bouillon cubes
2 stalks celery diced
1/2 green pepper diced
1 pimiento diced (or small jar red pimientos)
1 small can mushrooms drained, or
   equivalent of fresh mushrooms.

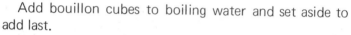

Add bouillon cubes to boiling water and set aside to add last.

Combine all ingredients in a Pam-sprayed casserole dish.

Add the above liquid and bake 350° for one hour until nicely browned. Be sure to use an extra thin bread with lesser calorie count.

FOOD FOR THOUGHT: "All I need to do is cry to him — oh, praise the Lord — and I am saved from all my enemies!" Psalms 18:3

CHEESE-TOPPED TUNA

244 calories per serving   Serves 1

1 slice bread
2 oz. drained and flaked tuna, water packed
1/4 cup warm asparagus, broccoli or green beans
1 oz. (1 slice) cheese

Toast bread. Lay tuna on slice.
Top with vegetables and then cheese.
Broil until cheese is melted and bubbly.

FOOD FOR THOUGHT: We want our house to be full of Christ — then we can taste HIS abundant banquet.

BAKED CODFISH WITH GRAPEFRUIT

113 calories per serving   Serves 4

1 12-oz. package frozen codfish
1 small grapefruit (or use canned grapefruit sections)
2 tablespoons grapefruit juice
2 tablespoons diet margarine
1/2 teaspoon salt
1/8 teaspoon pepper
paprika
1-1/2 teaspoons chopped parsley

Place fish in shallow baking dish.

Pour juice and margarine (melted) over fish. Sprinkle with salt, pepper and paprika. Bake 375° oven 30 minutes or until fish flakes easily.

Remove from oven. Place grapefruit sections atop fish; sprinkle with chopped parsley and bake 10 minutes longer.

FOOD FOR THOUGHT: Think what a privilege it is to have God listen to you.

LOBSTER CHUN KING

105 calories per serving   Serves 2 or 3

1 cup lobster meat
1 can bean sprouts
2 stalks chopped celery
2 slices onion
1 can mushroom slices, or fresh mushrooms
1 envelope chicken bouillon or cube

(add lobster last to the mixture . . . bake until tender)

FOOD FOR THOUGHT: The Lord came a long way to knock on your heart's door. If you don't open it, he is still in the tomb as far as you are concerned.

CHICKEN AND TURKEY

CHICKEN-A-LA-FRANCES

4 chicken breasts
2 cups fresh mushrooms
2 cups celery

2 cups onions
soy sauce
salt and pepper

FOR YOU:

Cut the chicken into small 1/4" strips, salt and pepper to taste, and stir fry in the bottom of a wok. For the skinnie minnie user, use soy sauce to stir fry. Put your chicken to one side, then stir fry your vegetables for just two or three minutes until they begin to appear transparent. Set yours aside in a small frying pan with a lid on it to keep it warm.

FOR THE REST OF YOUR FAMILY:

Roll their chicken strips in seasoned flour, and stir fry in oil. Then stir fry vegetables, and when the vegetables are done but crisp, put all ingredients back into the wok. There will be a small amount of liquid in the wok, so take 1/2 cup cream and stir into the liquid and vegetables. The flour which was cooked on the chicken will thicken the cream and the broth and make a fantastic gravy. Serve over rice and with either French fried noodles or slivered almonds.

Always remember, cook the vegetables first that need the longest cooking. Celery, then onions, then mushrooms. They need to be real crisp to be good.

For a change, add a little curry powder to the gravy. If you want to be extravagant, use a little curry powder and 1 teaspoon cream in yours.

Really a fabulous dinner!

FOOD FOR THOUGHT: The first thing you must do to become a Christian is to sin! Who hasn't qualified?

CHICKEN DELIGHT

126 calories per serving   Serves 4

4 chicken breasts, skin removed (3-oz. size)
2 cups bean sprouts
1 cup celery (tops and stalks cut in small pieces)
1/2 cup diced onions
1/2 green pepper cut in small pieces
1/2 cup red pepper cut in small pieces
2 chicken bouillon cubes

Cover breasts with water and bring to a boil, add 2 chicken bouillon cubes, simmer one hour. Add vegetables and cook until tender.

FOOD FOR THOUGHT: If we have fear in our lives, we aren't trusting God. "Thou shalt place no other gods before me." Do we put fear (Satan) above trust in God?

SHAKE & BAKE

to use on fish and chicken
162 calories entire recipe

2/3 cup dry skim milk
1 teaspoon salt
1/2 teaspoon pepper
1/2 teaspoon dry mustard
2 teaspoons paprika
2 teaspoons chicken bouillon
1 teaspoon poultry seasoning

FOOD FOR THOUGHT: Some people are not bad sinners, just consistent ones.

BAKED CHICKEN FOR FOUR

4 chicken breasts skin removed (3-oz. size)
Mix together 1 teaspoon ground ginger
1/3 teaspoon garlic powder
1 teaspoon salt
1/2 teaspoon pepper (approx.)

Mix seasonings together and rub chicken with mixture. Place in shallow baking dish, cover tightly with foil and bake 325° 1/2 hr. Then remove foil and broil chicken about 2 inches from heat until browned. Test for doneness.

FOOD FOR THOUGHT: When God withdraws his power, all earth and everything in it will disintegrate!

CHICKEN CACCIATORA

159 calories per serving   Serves 4

4 chicken breasts, skin removed (3-oz. size)
2 small green peppers
1 clove garlic
2 tablespoons finely chopped pimiento
1 bay leaf
1/8 teaspoon dried thyme
6 sprigs parsley or 1 tablespoon dried parsley
1 cup sliced raw mushrooms
2 cups stewed tomatoes

Simmer all ingredients together until tender. Serve over rice.

Add 76 calories per 1/2 cup serving of long-grain cooked rice.

FOOD FOR THOUGHT: "The Lord will not let a good man starve to death, nor will he let the wicked man's riches continue forever." Proverbs 10:3

"FIVE-SPICE" CHICKEN AND/OR TURKEY

Approximately 310 calories per serving   Serves 6

3 to 4 pound broiler-fryer chicken,
  cut into serving pieces
Marinate the chicken for approximately three hours
  in this soy sauce combination:
  1/2 cup soy sauce
  1/4 cup chopped onion
  1 clove garlic, crushed
  1 teaspoon minced fresh ginger root
  1/2 teaspoon cinnamon
  1/4 teaspoon each ground allspice and
    crushed anise seed (optional)
  1/8 teaspoon ground cloves
  pepper

Arrange chicken in shallow Pam-sprayed pan.

Mix the spices, sprinkle over chicken, and bake in 325°
oven about 45 minutes to 1 hour, test for tenderness,
turn once.

FOOD FOR THOUGHT: A self-made man is one who is in love
with his maker.

CHINESE CHICKEN

706 calories per serving   Serves 3

3 chicken breasts, skin and bone removed (3-oz. size)
  slice in 1/8-inch-thick slices.

Remove the ends and strings from 1/2 pound fresh peas.

Wash and slice 1/2 pound fresh mushrooms.

Cut green part of onions into 1-inch lengths and then slash both ends of 4 onions.

Slice 1 can (15 oz.) bamboo shoots, drained.

Arrange chicken and vegetables on tray.

1 tablespoon chicken stock dissolved in 1 cup water, or 1 cup regular-strength chicken broth.

Pour into small pitcher.

Mix together 1/4 cup soy sauce, 2 tablespoons corn-starch, 1/2 teaspoon each sugar and salt and pour into another small pitcher. This far in the recipe you have a total of 667 calories.

Place 1/2 cup salad oil and 1 package (4 oz.) cashew nuts in containers.

Arrange all of this together near fry pan. The oil and nuts = 1,450 calories!

Heat 1 tablespoon of the oil over moderate heat (350°), add nuts, shake pan until toasted, remove, set aside.

Add remaining oil to pan, add chicken, cook quickly, turning until it turns opaque.

Add peas and mushrooms; pour in broth, cover, and simmer two minutes.

Add bamboo shoots. Stir soy sauce mixture into the pan. Cook altogether until sauce is thickened, stir con-stantly. Simmer one minute uncovered. Mix in the green onions. Sprinkle with nuts and serve. (The nuts can be omitted as they are full of calories. Subtract 159 calories per serving if nuts omitted.)

WARNING:

This is a fabulous dinner for your family, but watch out for yourself. I only put it in here because it's so outstanding. It's sinful if you're losing weight, however. The oil of the Holy Spirit is much better for you.

FOOD FOR THOUGHT: SALTLESS "Christians"? = the Devil's Dump, so why be down in the dumps?

ROAST TURKEY IN PAPER BAG

Approximately 300 calories per serving

An 8 pound turkey will serve 10.

Prepare for cooking by rubbing with diet margarine, then sprinkle lightly with salt and flour. Put 1/2 teaspoon of salt inside cavity, along with an apple, orange, and onion, and 1/4 cup orange juice. Put the turkey into a large brown paper bag and roll the end up tightly. Place in roasting pan and set in 300° oven. You can forget it for four hours. When done, remove from oven and let stand for about 10 to 15 minutes. Then cut out top of bag and lift out the beautiful bird.

FOOD FOR THOUGHT: "Search me, O God, and know my heart; test my thoughts. Point out anything you find in me that makes you sad, and lead me along the path of everlasting life." Psalms 139:23-24

SANDWICHES

THE HISTORY OF THE
FRANCES HUNTER SALAD SANDWICH

Did you ever notice how God takes you long distances sometimes, to show you something new?

We were in New Zealand in 1976, had missed both lunch and supper, and couldn't find anyplace open to try to grab a "starvation" snack.

Room service was still available at our hotel, so we ordered sandwiches for four. When they arrived, I looked at them and decided they were about the skinniest sandwiches I'd ever seen! New Zealanders make their sandwiches on bread about 1/4 inch thick, so that makes them small to begin with, but these looked unusually thin.

I picked up the cover on one of them and discovered it had a thin coating of butter and a slice of cucumber! Thinking that the meat had slipped out of that section, I peeked at another — SAME THING! I kept looking until I discovered that they all contained the same thing — CUCUMBERS AND A LITTLE BUTTER!

We all decided to call the room service and see what had happened to the meat. When we asked if they had forgotten to put the meat on the sandwiches, there was a long pause, and suddenly a voice said, "Oh, that's right, you're Americans, aren't you?" I assured her we were and she said, "You do like meat on your sandwiches, don't you?" I never heard of anyone before who didn't eat meat or cheese, but . . . .

I had forgotten all about this until we were thinking about ways to keep your weight on an even level, or an easy way to lose a couple of pounds in the event you splurged a little somewhere along the line!

We remembered the thin-sliced bread in New Zealand, and were surprised to discover that our store had just started carrying the same type bread! Somehow or other, this was the start of the FRANCES HUNTER SALAD SANDWICH! We took what the New Zealanders had done, put little extra touches on it, and out came one of the most fantastic low-calorie sandwiches in the world, whether it be in New Zealand or America!

Try one right now, and you'll wonder how you ever lived so long without them.

Frances "layering" her salad sandwich!

FRANCES HUNTER SALAD SANDWICH

INGREDIENTS	CALORIES
1/2 teaspoon mayonnaise	17
6 slices cucumbers	5
1/4 firm tomato	10
1/4 onion	10
1/4 sliced green pepper	2
lettuce leaves	1
3 mushrooms, thinly sliced	5
1/8 large apple	10
1 kosher dill pickle	10
2 slices thin-sliced bread	70
	140

Charles and Frances making salad sandwiches on television program. The cameramen almost deserted their cameras to eat them! (The sandwiches, of course!)

This is one of the most fabulous sandwiches in the world! Wash all ingredients and slice as thin as you possibly can. Spread the mayonnaise as thin as possible on both pieces of bread. On one side lay 3 slices tomato and on the other 3 slices of onion. This allows the juice to run into the mayonnaise. Then start building your sandwich. Add the mushrooms on one side, cucumbers on the other. Be sure and sprinkle each layer with seasoned salt. Now add the pickle on one side, and green pepper on the other. On the green pepper side, put the thin slices of apple.

PRAY . . . this is one of the most important parts! Pray that when you put the sandwich together, it won't fly all over the ceiling or on the floor! Cut in half and you'll have a supersatisfying sandwich with only 140 calories involved.

You can also add raw crookneck squash if you like, or raw turnips. Either of these are delicious with very few calories. Another addition is a forkful of bean sprouts (drained). If you don't like the combination of the apple (I love it), leave it off.

If you have cut up more vegetables than you need for the sandwiches for you and your family, chop the leftovers very fine and use them in scrambled eggs the following morning. Sprinkle chili powder on top of the scrambled eggs.

FOR THE REST OF YOUR FAMILY: Those hearty eaters will enjoy this sandwich with a thick slice of roast beef, some bacon crumbles next to the tomato, sliced turkey, Swiss cheese, or any other kind of meat or cheese they enjoy. Use more mayonnaise on their sandwich, too.

FOOD FOR THOUGHT: Getting rid of ourself is like peeling an onion, layer by layer, and it is often a tearful process.

We're praying for you.

REUBEN SANDWICH

175 calories per serving   Serves 2

2 slices very thin bread
1 teaspoon mustard
caraway seed
1 cup sauerkraut, drained
2 oz. Swiss cheese slices

Spread toast with mustard, sprinkle with caraway seeds. Place cheese slices on bread and top with sauerkraut. Broil 4" from heat for about 4 minutes or until hot and light brown.

Be sure to drain and squeeze the sauerkraut, or you might have a "soggy" mess. I like this on rye bread.

FOOD FOR THOUGHT: Sin is such a sneaky little character that sometimes we do not even recognize it in the beginning for what it really is.

FRENCH STYLE TOAST

Approximately 65 calories per serving   Serves 1

Soak 1 slice bread in well-beaten egg. Put on piece of aluminum foil, sprinkle cinnamon on top. Add vanilla and sugar substitute in egg for sweeter taste. Slip under broiler. Watch carefully, and turn when brown.

Many times I eat pancakes or French toast with salt and pepper instead of something sweet. It's exciting and different this way.

FOOD FOR THOUGHT: The trouble with one sin is that it leads to another!

POPPY SEED ROLLS

50 calories per "roll"   Serves 10

Trim crusts of 10 very thin slices bread
Flatten each slice with rolling pin
Spread each with 1/2 teaspoon diet margarine and
  sprinkle with poppy seeds
Roll up, secure with toothpicks, place on
  Pam-sprayed baking sheet
Bake 425° until golden — about 10 minutes.
  Remove picks before serving.
    Super, but don't eat too many!

Try the same thing with sesame seeds. Add a little
Parmesan cheese for a flavor change. Your whole family
will love these.

FOOD FOR THOUGHT: Did you ever try to imagine how much
patience God must have had when you were first added to his
family?

LETTUCE LEAF SANDWICH

115 calories chicken or turkey,   Serves 1
125 for beef

Instead of bread, use large leaf of lettuce. Wrap around
small portion (3 oz.) turkey breast, 3 oz. chicken breast,
or lean beef.

FOOD FOR THOUGHT: The only person who is able to change
another person's disposition is Jesus Christ himself!

PIZZA SANDWICH

165 calories per serving   Serves 2

2 slices very thin bread
2 oz. Swiss or Muenster cheese
garlic powder
pinch oregano
4 teaspoons tomato juice
2 tablespoons canned mushrooms,
  or lots of fresh ones

Brown bread on one side under broiler. Turn and spread 2 teaspoons tomato juice on each. Sprinkle with garlic powder and oregano. Put cheese slices on top and sprinkle mushrooms over. Brown under broiler until cheese melts. Almost as good as the "real" thing, with lots less calories.

FOOD FOR THOUGHT: A miracle is the normal thing God does!

BEAN SPROUT, CHEESE AND
MUSHROOM TOAST TREAT

210 calories per serving   Serves 1

1 can bean sprouts, drained
1 slice American cheese
1 piece very thin toast, sprinkled lightly with garlic salt
  and Parmesan cheese
1/2 cup mushrooms

Drain sprouts, place in pie dish, put mushrooms on top and slice of cheese. Place under broiler until cheese becomes brown and bubbly. Serve with toast and soak up cheese sauce with toast. Super delicious, and a real satisfying one-dish luncheon or dinner.

FOOD FOR THOUGHT: Love your neighbor, it will drive him crazy!

DIET PIZZA

150 calories per serving   Serves 4

3 oz. lean ground beef
2 small garlic cloves, minced
2 tablespoons finely chopped onion
1 cup tomato juice
2 pinces each of oregano, basil, anise seeds,
  marjoram and rosemary
dash of cayenne pepper
2 tablespoons chopped parsley
salt and pepper to taste
4 slices thinly sliced bread, toasted
1 oz. grated Parmesan cheese
2 oz. grated Cheddar cheese

Brown ground beef in a non-stick frying pan. Add garlic and onion and sauté until golden. Drain off fat. Add remaining ingredients except bread and cheeses and simmer, uncovered, until sauce thickens. Stir occasionally to prevent sticking. When ready to serve, spoon sauce over toast and top with cheeses. Broil until bubbly.

You can dress this one up with a little green pepper cut into thin strips. Gives it an "extra" flavor. Mushrooms, too, are a real plus. Remember, only one slice of bread for you.

FOOD FOR THOUGHT: You can always be assured that God will do his part when you do your part!

SOUPS

FOOD FOR THOUGHT: "This being so, I want to remind you to stir into flame the strength and boldness that is in you, that entered into you when I laid my hands upon your head and blessed you. For the Holy Spirit, God's gift, does not want you to be afraid of people, but to be wise and strong, and to love them and enjoy being with them. IF YOU WILL STIR UP THIS INNER POWER, you will never be afraid to tell others about our Lord. . . ." 2 Timothy 1:6-8.

SOUPS

"Soup up" your body with soup! "Soup up" means to speed up (a motor or engine) by increasing the richness of the fuel mixture, or the efficiency of the fuel, so "soup up" your energy with a world of variety.

Soup is one of the greatest variables in the world because you can put anything in it, leave anything out, and it still tastes good. Probably the only thing I can think of that I personally wouldn't leave out, would be the lowly onion, which gives flavor to whatever else you put in. Now that I think of it, creamed cauliflower soup doesn't need it, but for the most part, an onion really adds zing to soup!

When it's a cold day, or when you're not feeling up to par, soup and a prayer are the best prescription I know. Or maybe you're one of those persons who likes to have a cold soup on a hot day. We're hot-soup eaters in our house, and I've included some of each, so whichever way you want it, you can find a Skinnie Minnie recipe to satisfy your taste buds!

For the rest of your family, after you take your portion out and keep it warm in a smaller pan, you might try adding dry spaghetti or rice to the vegetable soups. This will give body enough to satisfy the heartiest appetite! Note: My family loves what they call "Spaghetti Soup!"

If your family wants a big portion of meat along with soup, simmer the meat in a separate pan. I always use inexpensive chuck roast for this. Pour the soup over a generous serving of meat placed in soup bowl!

WARNING: Whenever you add beef, pork, chicken or fish, remember to add on the extra calories! Use caution, and increase flavor! Keep experimenting until you find the combination that's just right for you!

CABBAGE AND THINGS SOUP

73 calories per serving approximately   Serves 6

1/2 head cabbage, shredded
1 can French style green beans
1 can mushrooms (4 oz.)
1 can bean sprouts
1 48 oz. can tomato juice

Simmer until tender.
Other vegetables can
be added if desired —
parsley, onions, carrots.

FOOD FOR THOUGHT: Our mind is the receiver and storehouse of thoughts from the Holy Spirit.

ZUCCHINI SOUP

221 calories per serving   Serves 6

5 beef bouillon cubes
5 cups water
2 cloves garlic, minced
2 tablespoons butter
1-1/2 teaspoons leaf basil, crushed
1 teaspoon salt
1/8 teaspoon pepper
3 carrots, sliced
2 onions, chopped
1 lb. zucchini, diced
3 tomatoes, chopped
6 frankfruters, sliced

Simmer all ingredients together except zucchini, tomatoes and frankfurters until carrots are tender. Add remaining ingredients and cook until zucchini is tender.

This one is really unusual!

FOOD FOR THOUGHT: If you were perfect, you would have imperfection without submission to the will of God.

ASTONISHING ASPARAGUS

1 can asparagus with liquid
1 cup chicken bouillon
Salt
Pepper
Onion
Cayenne

Put canned asparagus and its liquid in the blender. Add the chicken bouillon. Puree. Season with salt, pepper, onion, any spice you like — bay leaf, cayenne. Delicious! Calories? Only 60.

FOOD FOR THOUGHT: The Christian life is like tea. Its full strength comes out when it's in hot water!

ITALIAN GAZPACHO (Cold Soup)

38 calories per serving   Serves 4

This is made with a tomato juice base (1 cup).
Add to this shredded fresh cucumbers (2 large), green peppers (2 large), celery chopped (1 cup), and seasonings to taste. Chill and serve cold. Keeps well for days in the refrigerator and is even better aged a few days.

Variations: onion chopped (1 large), tomatoes (4 large), beef consomme (1 can), Worcestershire sauce (3 tablespoons), oregano (1 tablespoon).

Our good friend Bob Murphy (author of <u>Christianity Rubs Holes In My Religion</u>) says, "This will fill you up to your earlobes!"

FOOD FOR THOUGHT: Don't become someone else's attitude by absorbing theirs, unless their attitude is good.

QUICK VEGETABLE SOUP

208 calories per serving   Serves 6

Saute in saucepan until brown:
    1 pound lean ground beef
Drain off all fat and stir in remaining ingredients:
    1 cup sliced carrots
    1 cup diced celery
    1 cub cubed, pared raw potatoes
    2 med. onions, chopped fine (about 1 cup)
    1 can tomatoes (28 oz.)
    2 teaspoons salt
    1 teaspoon bottled brown bouquet sauce
    1/4 teaspoon pepper
    1 bay leaf
    1/8 teaspoon basil
    3 cups water

Heat until boiling. Reduce heat. Cover and simmer just until vegetables are tender (about 20 minutes). Sometime add chili powder for a fabulous South-of-the-border flavor!

FOOD FOR THOUGHT: We have the right to refuse any of God's gifts, but he doesn't reserve the right to refuse us.

Recipes for vegetable soups are endless and many people sent in variations, and I've tried to take the one that seemed the best, and will make the following recommendation for things you can add to the above.
* 1/2 head cabbage, shredded — makes an unusual addition
* 1/2 fresh head of cauliflower, broken into tiny pieces
* Canned or fresh green beans
* Try oregano for a change of flavor
* Try adding clams sometime for clam chowder!
* What's wrong with green pepper (be careful, not too much!)

* Did you ever put Worcestshire sauce in soup?
* Try a little sage.
* Try a little dry mustard.
* I like thyme, too!
* Want something unusual — sprinkle a little nutmeg sometime!
* Use 4 whole peppercorns for flavor
* Curry powder in a chicken-based vegetable soup is unusual!

FOOD FOR THOUGHT: "Why spend your money on foodstuffs that don't give you strength? Why pay for groceries that don't do you any good? Listen and I'll tell you where to get good food that fattens up the soul!" Isaiah 55:2.

BEAN SPROUT SOUP

28 calories per serving   Serves 8

1 cup bean sprouts
1 cup green beans
1 carrot grated
3 dashes of dill weed
3 bouillon cubes (beef or chicken)
3 cups water
1 cup tomato juice
dash of garlic
1 pinch of Italian seasoning
1 small potato cubed

Boil together until ingredients are just tender. Serve with soy sauce if you like.

For that special surprise, add little pieces of pork which have been boiled with caraway seeds!

FOOD FOR THOUGHT: The modern word is "compromise;" the Bible calls it "lukewarm."

CREAMED CAULIFLOWER SOUP

18 calories per serving   Serves 4

Dissolve 2 packets instant chicken broth in 2 cups water.

Add one large head of cauliflower broken up.

Simmer until just tender. Place in blender and process at low speed.

Return to pan and reheat. Put chopped pimiento (red) on top.

If you feel daring, try a little jalapeno sauce on this!

FOOD FOR THOUGHT: "It is better to live in the corner of an attic than with a crabby woman in a lovely home." Proverbs 21:9

SUPER EASY TOMATO SOUP

1 can tomatoes, pureed in blender
water as needed
beef bouillon (4 cubes)
celery salt
seasoned salt
minced onion
lemon pepper
arrowroot to thicken

Charles likes Super Easy Tomato Soup because it's a "quickie" to fix. The amount of seasoning you put in is dependent upon your personal taste. Easy on the lemon pepper, though!

About 40 calories per cup.

For your family, make it Super Easy Cream of Tomato Soup by adding a little rich cream.

FOOD FOR THOUGHT: "It is better to eat soup with someone you love than steak with someone you hate." Proverbs 15:17.

VICHYSSOISE

106 calories per soup bowl serving   Serves 6

4 leeks, white part only (or onions)
1 tablespoon butter
3 potatoes, peeled and cubed
1 stalk celery chopped
2 sprigs parsley
4 cups chicken broth
2 cups skim milk
salt and pepper
pinch of nutmeg
finely chopped chives

Wash the leeks (or onions) well and slice thin.

Melt butter in heavy pan.

Add leeks (or onions), cover, cook over low heat until limp.

Add potatoes, celery, parsley, and chicken broth.

Simmer until potatoes are tender.

Put the mixture through a sieve or puree in an electric blender. Add milk, salt, pepper and nutmeg. Chill until icy cold. Serve with sprinkling of chopped chives.

You might not call it Vichyssoise if heated, but that's the way Charles likes it.

FOOD FOR THOUGHT: "The joy of the Lord is my strength."

CREAM OF MUSHROOM SOUP
121 calories entire recipe

1 4-oz. can or jar of mushrooms (save juice and use)
1 cup non-fat milk (liquid)
1 cube or envelope of beef bouillon
salt and pepper to taste

Blend altogether in blender.
Do not chop too fine.
Try adding fish to this sometime — you might be surprised! Boiled sole or haddock, flaked, are unusual! Add oregano while boiling.

FOOD FOR THOUGHT: The statute of limitation never runs out with Jesus.

CHILLED SPRING BORSCH
1 cup = less than 76 calories!   Serves 6

1 can diced beets
1-1/2 cups finely chopped peeled cucumber
1/4 cup minced onion (small onion)
1 qt. chilled buttermilk (1% fat)
1 teaspoon salt
1/2 teaspoon Worcestershire sauce
chopped parsley

Drain the beets. Combine all ingredients except parsley and chill. Serve in chilled bowls sprinkled with parsley. Makes about 6-1/2 cups.

FOOD FOR THOUGHT: "Winking at sin leads to sorrow; bold reproof leads to peace." Prov. 10:10.

FRESH SPINACH SOUP
(A European dish — from Macedonia, Yugoslavia)
Approximately 48 calories per serving   Serves 6

1 bag (10 oz.) fresh spinach (clean, trim ends off stems,
  cut spinach in half)
add 1-1/2 quarts water
2 tablespoons oil
1/2 teaspoon paprika
1/2 teaspoon salt
Cook for 1 hour, medium heat
Add 1/4 cup rice washed
Cook for 1/2 hour more or until rice cracks
Stir once in a while during cooking.

Try bacon or a little salt pork instead of the 2 table-spoons oil.

FOOD FOR THOUGHT: "I publicly praise the Lord for keeping me from slipping and falling." Psalms 26:12.

VEGETABLES
AND MAIN DISHES

Vegetables can be sad, and vegetables can be glad, depending upon what you put into them.

Life is exactly the same way, because it's what you put into life that regulates what you get out of it. If you put in just a little Jesus, you get a little in return. If you put in a lot of Jesus, you get a lot in return.

Vegetables can be the same thing day after day, and so can your own life unless you're willing to step out in faith and do what God wants you to do. Then it becomes an exciting challenge. Adding spice to your vegetables can perk them up, too!

Try some of these new recipes for food, and try some of the new recipes for living, too!

RICE WITH BEAN SPROUTS AND TOASTED SESAME SEEDS

217 calories per serving   Serves 4

3 tablespoons crushed toasted sesame seeds
2 minced green onions
1 clove garlic, minced or mashed
1 tablespoon salad oil or sesame oil
1-1/2 cups bean sprouts
2 cups hot cooked rice
2 tablespoons soy sauce

To toast the sesame seeds, place in a heavy frying pan, low heat. Stir until golden brown. Then crush by whirling in an electric blender or roll with rolling pin, or crush with pestle in a mortar.

Combine sesame seeds with onions and garlic and sauté in oil 3 minutes. Add bean sprouts and sauté until thoroughly hot. (It may be necessary to add a little water to keep ingredients from sticking.) Add hot rice and soy sauce and gently mix.

FOOD FOR THOUGHT: God never asks us to do anything that he hasn't already made a provision for the gifts to do them and the power to accomplish what he has called us for.

SLENDER SPAGHETTI

70 calories per serving   Serves 2

12 oz. tomato juice
small amount of artificial sweetener
garlic, salt, pepper, onions

Boil the above until thick. Serve over 2 cups bean sprouts which have been simmered gently until soft.

FOOD FOR THOUGHT: Carnality dwarfs spiritual growth.

CURRIED POTATO PATTIES

Approximately 96 calories per serving   Serves 4

2 cups hot mashed potatoes
1 egg
1/4 teaspoon curry powder
1 teaspoon chopped parsley
1 tablespoon diet margarine

Place the hot mashed potatoes in mixing bowl, add egg, curry powder, and parsley. Mix until blended. On Pam-sprayed baking sheet shape the mixture into patties and flatten slightly. Put dot of margarine in center. Bake 400° oven for 10 minutes or until heated through. (This is figuring potatoes mashed with small portion of milk.)

FOOD FOR THOUGHT: Contentment is learned.

SPINACH SOUFFLÉ

137 calories entire dish   Serves 1

1 cup chopped, cooked, drained spinach
2 tablespoons chopped onion cooked with spinach
1/4 cup cottage cheese (low-fat)
1 egg white, whipped

Mix spinach and onion with cottage cheese; fold in egg white. Pour into ungreased small baking dish. Bake 350° 20 to 25 min. Serves one. Could serve two with small servings (divide calories in half then).

FOOD FOR THOUGHT: Be loving!

CHINESE-STYLE DINNER

102 calories per serving   Serves 3

3 oz. finely chopped cooked chicken or pork
1-1/2 cups chicken broth
soy sauce, dry mustard, salt and pepper
4 stalks chopped celery
1/2 head cabbage, finely chopped (2 cups)
1/2 chopped onion
1 tablespoon cornstarch

Add broth to chicken or pork (bouillon cubes can be used to make broth). Season to taste and bring to boil. Lower heat and add celery, cabbage and onion. Cook until vegetables are transparent but still crisp. Mix cornstarch with water to make paste and add to mixture. Stir on low flame until sauce is thickened.

For variety try other vegetables such as cauliflower, broccoli and/or bean sprouts. (Calories figured using chicken. Calorie count can be lessened by using diet chicken broth.)

FOOD FOR THOUGHT: God never fails.

CORN MEDLEY

126 calories per approximately
   10 oz. servings   Serves 4

1 10-oz. pkg. frozen whole corn
1/2 cup chopped celery
1 chicken bouillon cube crushed
1 12-oz. can sliced mushrooms, drained
1 med. tomato cut in wedges
1/3 cup water

Combine all ingredients
and simmer 5 to 7 min.

FOOD FOR THOUGHT: God can solve all the problems that you can't.

PANNED CABBAGE

Approximately 32 calories per serving   Serves 2 or 3

1/2 teaspoon butter flavoring
1/2 cup water
1 teaspoon instant bouillon
3 cups shredded cabbage

Bring water, bouillon and flavoring to a boil. Add cabbage. Cover. Simmer gently, stir once in awhile. Cook 10-15 min.

FOOD FOR THOUGHT: God is!

STIR-FRIED ASPARAGUS

Approximately 63 calories per serving   Serves 4

About 2 pounds fresh asparagus. Snap off tough ends. Cut in thin slanting slices. Drop into boiling salted water. Pre-cook until barely tender (about 2 minutes). Drain. Cool and set aside.

Heat a frying pan or wok over high heat and put in 1 tablespoon salad oil, 1 clove garlic, minced, 1 teaspoon finely chopped fresh ginger (optional), 1 tablespoon water, the equivalent of 1 teaspoon sugar substitute, about 1/2 teaspoon salt. Add asparagus, water, sugar, and salt. Keep turning with spatula until heated through (about 1 minute). Turn onto warm serving dish. Garnish with parsley and snipped green onions.

(Most vegetables can be stir-fried in this manner. Try broccoli, bean sprouts, brussel sprouts, carrots, squash, etc.)

FOOD FOR THOUGHT: Drinking from the fountain of life is far more satisfying than any other kind of drink!

BEAUTIFUL BEETS

111 calories per serving (approximate)   Serves 1

Cook 1 cup beets, frozen, or canned with 2 table-spoons unsweetened concentrated orange juice. Artificial sweetener to taste. Add a dash of nutmeg. Very, very good and certainly unusual.

FOOD FOR THOUGHT: Thank you, Lord, for letting me accept myself as you see me, and not as I might see myself.

BRAISED CELERY AU GRATIN

Approximately 35 calories per serving   Serves 4

1 pound bunch celery
3/4 cup consomme
1/2 teaspoon Worcestershire
salt and pepper to taste
2 tablespoons diet margarine, melted
grated Parmesan cheese

Cut off the root end of the celery, separate stalks, cut off leaves. Wash stalks well, remove tough strings. Slash into even lengths. Place in large skillet, along with the consomme and Worcestershire. Cover and cook gently until just tender. Remove to shallow baking dish. Sprinkle with salt, pepper, melted margarine, and grated Parmesan cheese. Broil or bake until cheese is melted.

FOOD FOR THOUGHT: When we satisfy God, we are only then truly satisfied.

CABBAGE COMBINATION

Approximately 80 calories per serving   Serves 4

2 slices bacon, fry, drain and crumble
Combine with: 1 med. head cabbage, finely shredded
            1/2 green pepper, finely chopped
            1 onion, finely chopped
            3 stalks celery, finely chopped
            2 teaspoons imitation butter-flavored salt

Simmer altogether for 2-3 minutes,
  stirring all the while.
Add: 2 cups stewed tomatoes
                1 4-oz. can drained mushrooms

Continue cooking until all warmed through and tender.

FOOD FOR THOUGHT: "Trust in your money and down you go!
Trust in God and flourish as a tree!" Proverbs 11:28

FRANKS AND GREEN BEANS

259 calories per serving   Serves 6

Brown 1 pound franks cut in two-inch pieces.
Remove franks from skillet.
Cook 1 cup diced celery, 1/2 cup diced onions in 1/2 cup chicken broth.
Add 9 oz. frozen French style green beans, 1-1/2 cups tomato juice, 1/4 cup water, 1/2 teaspoon sugar substitute, 1 tablespoon vinegar, 2 teaspoons prepared mustard.
Simmer 30 minutes stirring occasionally.

FOOD FOR THOUGHT: Do you run on batteries, or are you plugged in?

GREEN BEANS VINEGRETTE

38 calories per serving   Serves 2

1 can French cut green beans
1/4 onion sliced in thin curves
1 tablespoon vinegar
1 beef bouillon cube

Place onion in saucepan with beef bouillon and 1 cup water until onion is transparent. Add other ingredients. Simmer until hot. Season with celery salt, lemon butter and/or butter-flavored salt. (This is just as good served cold.)

FOOD FOR THOUGHT: God's retirement plan — Heaven!

BAKED POTATO WEDGES

Approximately 100+ calories   Serves 1

Cut medium potatoes lengthwise into wedges. Brush sides with beaten egg white. Sprinkle with Parmesan cheese and oregano. Bake 425° 25 min.

FOOD FOR THOUGHT: God gives promises to both good men and evil men; and he keeps his promise to both!

BAKED POTATO A LA TOMATO

168 calories   Serves 1

After baking whole potato, cut your baked potato open and soften it with a fork. Pour the following over it and put back in the oven until warm: 2 canned tomatoes diced with a dash of oregano. Salt and pepper and a little garlic if desired. Really super. (Use diet whole canned tomatoes only 39 calories.)

FOOD FOR THOUGHT: Christians have to drink out of saucers because their cups runneth over.

STEW FOR TWO

126 calories per serving   Serves 2

2 cups water
2 beef bouillon cubes
1/4 head cabbage (wedge) or more if desired
2 potatoes
2 turnips
1 carrot
salt & pepper to taste
Simmer until tender.

FOOD FOR THOUGHT: Be forgiving!

SALAMI POTATOES

One potato = 90 calories

Take a raw well-scrubbed white potato (5-1/2—6 oz.). Cut into slices (as if you were cutting salami), leaving the skin on. Put the slices on a cookie sheet and top with garlic salt, salt and pepper, herbs, or whatever you like. Then put under the broiler for about five minutes or so (depending on your oven and tastes).

Delicious as snacks or served with meals. Even the non-Daniel fasters like them.

FOOD FOR THOUGHT: "Fire goes out for lack of fuel, and tensions disappear when gossip stops." Proverbs 26:20

SPINACH-FILLED BAKED POTATOES

229 calories per serving   Serves 4

4 med.-sized baking potatoes, baked
1/4 cup diet margarine
1 teaspoon salt
1/2 teaspoon sugar
1/2 teaspoon dill weed
1/4 teaspoon pepper
1 pkg. (10 oz.) frozen, chopped spinach thawed
1/4 cup chopped chives (fresh, frozen, or freeze-dried)
1/4 cup grated Parmesan cheese

Slit each potato lengthwise down the center after baking and carefully scoop out inside, leaving the potato skin shell. Set shells aside. Place potatoes into large bowl of electric mixer and add margarine, salt, sugar, dill, and pepper. Beat at medium speed until blended. Squeeze excess moisture from spinach and add with chives to potatoes, blending well. Refill shells. Bake, uncovered, in 350° oven for about 30 minutes or until heated through. Remove from oven and sprinkle each potato with cheese.

FOOD FOR THOUGHT: Turn your desires toward making your marriage an exciting one, and see what happens right in front of your own eyes.

VEGETABLE TERIYAKI

45 calories per serving if six served   Serves 4-6

1/2 cup sliced onions
4 cups green beans
2 cups bean sprouts (fresh if possible)
1/2 cup sliced mushrooms
3 tablespoons soy sauce
    Cook to desired tenderness.

FOOD FOR THOUGHT: Life is not a problem to be solved, but a mystery to be lived.

BAKED POTATO STUFFED WITH COTTAGE CHEESE

168 calories per serving   Serves 3

3 baked med. potatoes
1/2 cup skim milk
1 cup diet cottage cheese
salt, pepper, paprika

Cut potato in half lengthwise after baking.

Scoop out inside. Mash and beat in skim milk.

Add cottage cheese and seasonings. Sprinkle with paprika.

Return to oven and bake 400° until brown.

FOOD FOR THOUGHT: More things are wrought by prayer than this world dreams of.

POTATO TOMATO POT

93 calories per serving   Serves 4

2 med. potatoes, cut up
1 med. tomato, cut up
1 med. onion, sliced
3/4 teaspoon salt
dash pepper
1 tablespoon olive oil

In small baking dish, toss vegetables, salt and pepper with oil. Cover and bake 350° for 30 min. Uncover and bake (to brown) until tender.

FOOD FOR THOUGHT: Prayer should be the key of the day and the lock of the night.

CURRIED VEGETABLE STEW

48 calories per serving   Serves 4

1/2 cup sliced onions
2 cups sliced zucchini squash
3 med. tomatoes (wedged)
1/4 teaspoon salt
1/4 teaspoon curry powder
1/4 teaspoon ginger
dash pepper
   Cook until tender, but still crisp.

FOOD FOR THOUGHT: Where God guides, God provides.

STREAMLINED STEW

130 calories per serving   Serves 1
(without meat added)

1 medium size potato
1 medium size onion
   Dice onion and potato in fourths. Put in piece of foil
and sprinkle package of bouillon (or a bouillon cube) and
half cup of water (make high sides). Close up tight and
bake for about an hour. Super delightful, and super low
in calories. For a change put a little chili pepper on top of
the potato and onion. If you want a meaty flavor, add
about 1/8 pound hamburger and see what happens.
   Put two or three cubes of beef in for the meat in your
menu. You can regulate the calories by the amount of
beef you put in!

FOOD FOR THOUGHT: It's not a sin never to win someone to
Christ, but it's a sin not to try!

BAKED ACORN SQUASH

93 calories per serving   Serves 2

Cut acorn squash in half. Remove seeds. Fill centers with 4 tablespoons unsweetened orange juice. Sprinkle liberally with diet brown sugar, add 1 teaspoon diet oleo, dash nutmeg or cinnamon. Bake 375° until tender, approx. 1 hour. (Use med. size squash.)

FOOD FOR THOUGHT: "Wisdom is a tree of life to those who eat her fruit; happy is the man who keeps on eating it." Proverbs 3:18

LET'S TRY OVEN-FRYING

When I discovered the caloric content of fried foods, I discarded them 100%, but there is that time when you would like to have something that at least tastes like it's fried. Then I came up with "oven-frying," a simple, uncomplicated way to "fry" foods without involving yourself with deep-fat, smoke and a messy kitchen.

Did you know you can come up with a different fish or chicken dinner that tastes as good as when it's French-fried? Whenever I think of fat containing 1,945 calories per cup, and how much can be soaked up in a piece of French-fried chicken, or fish, I praise God for the oven.

It's so easy once you find the little secret. You have to have some kind of oil in order to be able to get a crunch coating on the outside, but most meats and chicken have enough fat to do the job. Did you know the more you cook fried foods, and the thicker the coating, the more calories are absorbed into the dish? Did you know that frying can double or triple the calorie count of many foods that are non-fattening?

Turn your oven on real high, because you have to cook oven-fried food fast. When the crust becomes a beautiful color on the outside, check the inside to see if it's done.

Try some of these and see if you don't think they're fabulous.

TAHITIAN PORK CHOPS OR CHICKEN

265 calories per serving   Serves 4

4 lean pork chops or four chicken breasts
2-1/2 tablespoons soy sauce
1/8 teaspoon ground ginger
1/2 teaspoon garlic powder
1 egg
4 tablespoons packaged bread crumbs

Combine the soy sauce, egg, ginger and garlic powder.
Place bread crumbs in paper bag. Dip pork chops into egg mixture, then shake in crumb mixture, seeing that the chicken or pork chops are evenly coated.

Spray a flat pan with Pam and then lay pork chops in pan.

Cook 30 minutes at 350°, then turn and bake 20 minutes longer.

Do not overcook! Really super.

FOOD FOR THOUGHT: God WANTS — the devil WONT'S!

OVEN-FRIED HADDOCK

About 225 calories per serving   Serves 2

1/2 pound fresh or frozen haddock
 (sole is good, so is flounder)
4 tablespoons packaged bread crumbs
2 tablespoons mayonnaise
1/4 teaspoon salt
1/4 teaspoon pepper
paprika or chili powder for color

Spray baking dish with Pam. Put crumbs in bag. Spread mayonnaise thinly on each piece of fish and shake in bag, coating evenly. Place in baking dish and bake for 8 minutes in 450° oven. Do not overcook because you'll dry the fish out. Sprinkle salt, pepper and chili powder or paprika on, and garnish with thin slices of lemon or lime. Really crisp and crunchy.

FOOD FOR THOUGHT: Obedience to God is the key to abundant life.

TURKEY OR VEAL

About 265 calories per serving

Use the same recipe as for the oven-fried haddock, but bake only 15 minutes, turning once, in a 400° oven.

FOOD FOR THOUGHT: "Men ought to wash other men's feet!"

BAKED-FRIED DRUMSTICKS

170 calories per serving   Serves 2

4 chicken drumsticks
1 tablespoon orange juice
3 tablespoons seasoned bread crumbs
1/4 teaspoon seasoned salt
pepper to taste
paprika to color

Rub drumsticks with orange juice. Put bread crumbs, salt, pepper and paprika in paper bag, add chicken and shake well.

Lay chicken in baking dish and bake in a very hot oven 450° for 30 minutes, without turning, or until it is crispy and crunchy.

FOOD FOR THOUGHT: Instead of thinking to yourself, try "thinking to God."

BAKED-FRIED-EGGPLANT

About 90 calories per serving   6 servings to 1 eggplant

I loved fried eggplant, but it can probably soak up more oil than any other vegetable, but this recipe gives you the same flavor without your having a guilt feeling about eating and enjoying something that really looks like it's French-fried.

Slice eggplant into 1/2-inch slices, dip in 5 tablespoons low-calorie dressing, either Romano or Italian. Shake in paper bag with bread crumbs until well coated. Sprinkle small amount of Parmesan cheese on the top, and bake for 8 minutes in 475° oven, then turn and bake for an additional 5 minutes. Fantastic!

FOOD FOR THOUGHT: To me, every minute of every day and night is an unspeakable, perfect miracle.

SALADS AND
SALAD DRESSINGS

Heavenly Decapod
Crustaceans in an
Angel Nest of Lettuce
(Shrimp Salad)

SALADS

HEAVENLY DECAPOD CRUSTACEANS IN AN ANGEL NEST OF LETTUCE

(Fancy name for a simple shrimp salad)

150 calories per serving   Serves 1

1 can medium deveined shrimp   Lettuce bed
10 cucumber slices   5 mushrooms, sliced
sliced onion rings
tomatoes (10 small pieces)
10 slivers green pepper

This salad is one of the most beautiful ever to serve at a luncheon or light dinner.

On it, I like the lettuce bed chopped up instead of broken. It absorbs the flavor of the shrimp better.

Make sure the canned shrimp has been thoroughly washed and drained so that no fishy taste remains. Soak in ice cubes for approximately 20 minutes before serving so the shrimp are firm.

While shrimp are soaking in ice cubes, score the cucumber with fork tines, and slice diagonally. Place 10 slices around the edges of a dinner plate. Fill inside with bed of lettuce. Place shrimp on top of lettuce bed, and garnish each piece of cucumber with a small wedge of tomato. Slice white sweet onions into thin slices and break apart to lay over top of shrimp for lacy pattern. Lay mushrooms, fanned out, on salad. (See picture) Put sliver of crisp green pepper between each cucumber slice.

Serve with lemon juice and soy sauce, or red sauce for your family who don't have to worry about weight. Any kind of dressing is delicious. Fresh shrimp is fabulous, but I keep canned shrimp on hand for emergency occasions.

Serve with saltines or rye crackers. WARNING! Four saltines have 50 calories.

FOOD FOR THOUGHT: Faith is the bridge between hope and reality.

MOCK POTATO SALAD

66 calories per cup   Serves 4 or 5

2 10-oz pkg. frozen cauliflower, or 1 head fresh cauliflower
  cooked until tender, drained and mashed

Add: 2 stalks celery, diced

               1/2 green pepper, chopped

               1 large dill pickle, chopped or

                2 tablespoons pickle relish

Dressing: 3 tablespoons prepared mustard

               1 teaspoon onion, minced fine, or

                onion flakes

               1 teaspoon chopped parsley

               1 teaspoon salt

               1/2 teaspoon lemon juice

               2 teaspoons Worcestershire sauce

               enough low-calorie salad dressing to moisten,

                and add artificial sweetener to taste

  Be sure to use a cutting board.

  Pour over "salad" ingredients, blend well and chill. Enjoy!

FOOD FOR THOUGHT: Train your face by turning the corners of
your mouth up into a smile. Train your appetite so your food
smiles at your body needs.

SPARKLING SPINACH SALAD

About 85 calories per serving   Serves 1

Large bowl of freshly washed spinach
6 mushrooms, sliced
bacon crumbles (1 slice of bacon, fried and crumbled)
reducer's salad dressing
1/4 sliced onion (thinly sliced)
salt & pepper

FOR YOU:

Place the fresh spinach (as much as you want) into a large salad bowl, arrange the 6 sliced mushrooms over one half of the bowl, then sprinkle the bacon crumbles on the other half. Pour 1 tablespoon reducer's salad dressing over entire salad.

Pull the onion apart and lay the onion rings in a lacy design over the entire top. It's especially pretty with a purple onion.

For a change, leave off the bacon crumbles and add Mandarin orange slices. Believe it or not, be sure to leave the onion rings on because the flavor is really unusual and satisfying!

FOR YOUR FAMILY — add any extra goodies you want to, such as blue cheese dressing (or any other dressing they enjoy), grated swiss cheese, grated ham, or more bacon. Almonds are a delicious extra, too.

FOOD FOR THOUGHT: PRAY-s the Lord!

MARINATED CAULIFLOWER OR
MUSHROOM SALAD

102 calories per serving   4 servings

Wash quart of mushrooms, leave whole, or
break head of cauliflower into flowerets and slice thinly

six green onions, chopped with tops
1 carrot, chopped
marinate overnight in low-fat French Dressing, just barely
  enough to moisten (about 1 cup). Stir once or twice.

Just before serving, add: 1/2 avocado, 2 medium
tomatoes (chopped), 1 teaspoon salt, 1/2 teaspoon
pepper. Toss very well. Serve on bed of crisp lettuce. If
you don't have tomatoes, try a few pieces of pimiento.
The mushrooms are my favorite!

FOOD FOR THOUGHT: When you "marinate" something, it
means to let it stay in a mixture of ingredients until it soaks up and
becomes the nature of the marinade. We all need to be "marinated" in Jesus, and stay there long enough to soak up his nature.

COTTAGE CHEESE SPECIAL

95 calories per serving   Serves 2

2/3 cup cottage cheese mixed   Put all ingredients in
  with 1/2 cup skim milk   blender at high speed
1 tablespoon paprika and salt   for 10 seconds. Serve
  to taste   this on salad greens.
2 tablespoons lemon juice
1/2 garlic clove
1/2 green pepper, chopped fine
4 radishes, chopped fine

FOOD FOR THOUGHT: No need to trust the outcome — trust
God!

MARINATED GREEN SALAD

140 calories per serving   Serves 6

1 9-oz. pkg. frozen artichoke hearts
1 10-oz. pkg. frozen peas

Cook these two according to directions on package.
Drain well and add:

1 cup diagonally sliced celery
1/2 cup chopped green onions
1/4 cup vegetable oil
1/4 cup cider vinegar
1 teaspoon salt
1/4 teaspoon black pepper
romaine leaves or other salad greens,
    torn into bite-size pieces

Combine all ingredients in medium size bowl. Cover.
Refrigerate one hour or until well chilled. Stir occasionally. Line serving dish with the romaine and spoon on
the marinated mixture.

FOOD FOR THOUGHT: Who would ever think of artichokes and
peas? Who would ever think of Jesus and a sinner? Put them
together and you have something wholesome and good!

PINEAPPLE AND COTTAGE CHEESE TREAT SALAD

70 calories per serving   Serves 8

3 cups diet-pack pineapple tidbits drained
3/4 cup skim cottage cheese
1/4 cup orange juice

Blend all three ingredients together. Chill well and
serve on lettuce leaves. Put fresh strawberry on top.

FOOD FOR THOUGHT: Giving our life means LIVING his life!

THREE TAKE-YOUR-PICK SAUERKRAUT SALADS
(Each has a definite place)
Low calories in all — from 29 to 43   Serves 6

1 16-oz. can sauerkraut
2 cups celery, chopped
1 sweet bell pepper, chopped
1/2 cup pimiento, chopped
2 teaspoons artificial sweetener (or equivalent in regular
  sugar may be used)

Mix all ingredients
  together well.
Cover and refrigerate
  overnight.

1 1-lb. can sauerkraut
1/2 cup sugar
1 medium green pepper
2 stalks celery
1 medium onion
1/2 cup grated carrots

Drain sauerkraut; rinse with cold water if desired. Combine sauerkraut and sugar and let stand while preparing remaining ingredients. Dice the green pepper, celery and onion. Add to sauerkraut mixture along with the carrots and blend well. Refrigerate the mixture overnight before serving.

1 32-oz. can sauerkraut
1 onion, finely chopped
1 green pepper, finely chopped
2 cups diced celery
2-3 tablespoon liquid artificial sweetener
1/4 cup vinegar

Combine all ingredients and mix well. Refrigerate for at least 24 hours before serving.

FOOD FOR THOUGHT: Father, Son and Holy Ghost — we need all three, because each has a definite place.

THE SHAPE-UP SALAD BOWL

200 calories per serving   Serves 2

1 can (6-1/2 or 7 oz.) water-
  packed tuna, drained and flaked
1-1/3 cups bean sprouts, drained
1 medium green pepper, cut in
  strips
2 pimientos, cut in strips
4 green onions
2 mushrooms, sliced
2 hard-cooked eggs, sliced
lettuce
parsley and dill weed

Arrange salad ingredients in lettuce-lined bowl. Garnish with the parsley and egg slices. Sprinkle dill over egg slices.
Serve with your favorite low-calorie dressing and prepare to count on flavor, not calories.

To "shape up" means "to develop to a definite form, condition, etc.; to develop satisfactorily or favorably."

FOOD FOR THOUGHT: Paul spent a lifetime telling people to "shape up" to the definite form of Jesus Christ! Not only do we need to "shape up" our physical bodies, but our spiritual bodies as well.

BACON-CURRY SLAW

65 calories per serving   Serves 4 to 6

6 to 8 cups finely shredded red
  and green cabbage
1/3 cup diet mayonnaise
2 tablespoon cider vinegar
1 teaspoon salt
1/4 teaspoon each pepper and
  curry powder
1 tablespoon sugar
4 slices bacon, cooked crisp

Stir together the mayonnaise with all ingredients except cabbage and bacon. Now pour the dressing over cabbage and coat thoroughly. Crumble bacon over slaw and mix lightly.

FOOD FOR THOUGHT: You cannot give God second place — he has no place to live unless he has first place in our lives.

TUNA SALAD WITH BEAN SPROUTS
202 calories per serving   Serves 2

1 can (6-1/2 or 7 oz.) water-
  packed tuna, flaked
3/4 cup fresh bean sprouts
3 teaspoons capers (optional)
1/4 cup diet mayonnaise
1 teaspoon soy sauce
2 whole sweet midget pickles

Gently stir ingredients together, except pickles. Line salad plates with lettuce leaves. Mound tuna mixture on lettuce. Slice pickles lengthwise and place atop tuna with cherry tomato in center.

FOOD FOR THOUGHT: There's something special about tuna fish and sweet pickles. There's something super special about the Christian life!

TWO-TONE SALAD
62 calories per serving   Serves 4

1/2 medium head lettuce, cut-up
3 cups cut-up spinach
2 hard-cooked eggs, sliced
1/2 cup minced onion

Toss salad together lightly, or layer, light and dark. Put eggs on top with minced onions.

Heat your favorite low-calorie dressing for a different flavor. Try adding a few bacos to the heated dressing too.

FOOD FOR THOUGHT: God gives us his strength, after we give him ours.

CHRISTIAN COLESLAW

40 calories per 1/2 cup   Serves 4

Grate or shred 1 small head of cabbage (2 cups)
Shred 1 carrot
1 stalk celery, chopped fine (or use 1/2 teaspoon celery seed)
2 tablespoons onion chopped fine
Dressing: 1 tablespoon vinegar
               2 packages sugar substitute
               2 tablespoons dry powdered milk (low-fat)
               1 tablespoon mayonnaise (if diet mayonnaise
               is used, calorie count is considerably lower)

For special occasions when you don't have company coming over, you might add a little garlic flavor for a special treat! I always let it sit for several hours, if possible. The flavor really soaks in much better.

FOOD FOR THOUGHT: Soak up the word of God, and you'll feel better!

THE "SAD" SALAD
(Wilted Lettuce)

56 calories per serving   Serves 4
"When I am sad, He makes me glad!"

Fry 3 slices of bacon real crisp, then crumble. Drain off most of the fat, stir in 1/2 cup mild vinegar, salt and pepper, 1 teaspoon brown sugar. Pour hot dressing over coarsely shredded lettuce (two small or one large head of lettuce). Crumble bacon over top.

I ate this as a little child because we couldn't afford salad dressing. Today I eat it because it's delicious and low calorie!

FOOD FOR THOUGHT: Jesus makes me glad!

TUNA TEMPTATION

72 calories per serving Serves 4

2 6-1/2-oz. cans of water-packed tuna, drained and flaked
1-1/2 cups cherry tomatoes, halved
1/2 med. onion, sliced and broken into rings
1 med. cucumber sliced thin
1/2 cup sliced celery
8 cups torn lettuce

Mix above ingredients. Over this, pour the dressing:

3/4 cup light vinegar
2 teaspoons sugar = 30 calories (subtract 26 calories if sugar
 substitute is used instead)
1-1/2 dried basil leaves crushed

salt and pepper to taste

FOOD FOR THOUGHT: This is one kind of temptation you don't have to ask God to give you strength to overcome. This one you can enjoy wholeheartedly!

APPLE-CELERY CONCOCTION

126 calories per serving (without mayonnaise) Serves 1
Add 16 calories for 1 tablespoon diet mayonnaise.

1/2 apple sliced
1/2 cup celery diced
1/2 banana (optional)
1 tablespoon grape-nuts

Moisten ingredients with
diet mayonnaise
sufficient to hold
together.

FOOD FOR THOUGHT: Mix faith and action to get results.

STUFFED CUCUMBER APPETIZER

14 calories per one-inch slice (filled)   Serves 12

2 slender cucumbers
1/2 cup cottage cheese, low-fat
2 green onions, minced
1/4 cup finely cut celery
1/2 teaspoon dill weed, tarragon
  or marjoram leaves
1/4 teaspoon salt
pepper to taste, minced parsley,
  watercress (optional)

Peel cucumbers, run fork tines down sides of peeled cucumber. Cut in 1-inch slices. Scoop out part of insides to form a little cup-like area. Combine other ingredients and fill cucumber cups. Sprinkle with parsley, etc.

FOOD FOR THOUGHT: You can only put as much into the cucumber as you have scooped out. God can only fill us as much as we empty ourselves!

MIXED VEGETABLE SALAD

71 calories per serving   Serves 6

1 pkg. (10 ozs.) frozen mixed vegetables,
  cooked and drained
1/2 cup diced celery
1/4 cup minced onion
1/4 cup sour cream substitute
1/4 cup bottled bleu cheese dressing low-fat
dash of Worcestershire sauce
salt and pepper to taste
salad greens torn into bite-size pieces

Different — you might like it! And you'll never know until you try. The same thing is true of Christianity — you never know how good it is until you try it!

FOOD FOR THOUGHT: When your eyes are fixed on Jesus you don't have time to see faults in others.

YOGURT CUCUMBER SALAD
100 calories per serving   Serves 2

Salad:	2 unpeeled cucumbers, sliced thin
	1/4 cup onions (preferably sweet),
	thinly sliced
	1-1/2 teaspoon salt
Dressing:	2 tablespoons chopped parsley
	3/4 teaspoon dill weed
	1/8 teaspoon garlic salt
	1 cup plain yogurt

Before adding dressing to salad, drain cucumbers and onions well. Stir in dressing. Chill 30-45 minutes, tossing occasionally.

FOOD FOR THOUGHT: Life is too short to cheat on our tax return or our food promises, and eternity is too long.

SHRIMP SURPRISE
190 calories   1 serving

1 small can tiny, drained shrimp
1 small can asparagus pieces
1 tablespoon dried celery
1 tablespoon chopped chives
1 tablespoon lemon juice
1 tablespoon soy sauce (optional)
salt and pepper
Mix and let sit for short time.

Serve in scooped out tomato. Different flavor!

FOOD FOR THOUGHT: Love doesn't know what a dollar sign is.

ANGELED EGGS

75 calories per serving   Serves 4

4 hard-boiled eggs
1 tablespoon tomato juice
1-1/2 teaspoons vinegar
1 teaspoon minced onion
1/2 teaspoon salt
1/8 teaspoon pepper
1/8 teaspoon liquid artificial sweetener
dash of chili powder or
1/4 teaspoon celery seeds

Cool and shell eggs; cut longways. Blend all the ingredients and pile yolk mixture into egg whites.

FOOD FOR THOUGHT: Why should the devil always get the credit for something as good as this!

MOLDED VEGETABLE SALAD

168 calories for entire salad

Sprinkle 2 envelopes gelatine on 3/4 cup tomato juice. Heat until dissolved. Stir in 1/4 cup tomato juice, 1/2 teaspoon salt, and 1/2 cup red vinegar (opt. 1/4 teaspoon tabasco).

Cool until slightly thickened.

Fold in vegetables: 1/2 cup diced green pepper, 1/2 cup chopped onion (sweet red), 1 tablespoon chives.

Refrigerate until firm. Serve on lettuce leaf.

FOOD FOR THOUGHT: It's not what people are doing in the Christian world that makes Christian news; it's what God is doing in people. Hallelujah!

LIME-PINEAPPLE SALAD

60 calories per serving   Serves 4

Pour 2 tablespoons dietetic lemon-lime soda pop into 1 quart bowl.

Sprinkle 1 envelope unflavored gelatine over soda pop and allow to soften.

Heat balance of 2 cups dietetic lemon-lime soda pop in pan and bring to a boil.

Combine with gelatine mixture. Dissolve thoroughly.

Add 1/2 teaspoon lime juice, few drops green food coloring. Place in refrigerator until partially set.

Add 2/3 cup low-fat cottage cheese and 1/2 cup crushed pineapple with juice.

Mix well altogether and place in refrigerator until firm. Serve on lettuce leaves.

FOOD FOR THOUGHT: Our desire to be like Jesus separates us from sin.

CARROT AND COTTAGE CHEESE SALAD

60 calories per serving   Serves 6

Cover 6 individual salad plates with crisp watercress or lettuce, or both.

Place 1/2 cup grated carrots in center of greens.

Blend 6 tablespoons skim cottage cheese with 1/2 teaspoon curry powder, form into 12 small balls and place 2 balls on each plate.

Pour dressing made of 6 tablespoons yogurt and 1 small onion, finely chopped, over salad.

Make your salad look attractive!

FOOD FOR THOUGHT: Worry makes us unattractive to others and to God.

THREE-WAY SALAD

103 calories per serving   Serves 4

1 can pineapple — drained (save liquid)
1 orange
1 banana
1 envelope gelatin
2/3 cup dry non-fat milk
1/2 teaspoon vanilla

Add enough water to pineapple juice to equal 1 cup. Dissolve gelatin in 1/2 cup of juice. Heat to dissolve gelatin. Remove from heat and cool, partially. Add milk, vanilla and 16 drops of liquid sweetener. Beat 10 minutes until stiff. Add pineapple, orange and banana. Refrigerate.

FOOD FOR THOUGHT: This salad is so heavenly tasting, you'd think it must be sinful, but it's not, so enjoy yourself!

LOW-CALORIE BEAN SALAD

24 calories per serving   Serves 5

1 16-oz. can green or wax beans, drained
1 green pepper, finely chopped
1 medium onion, thinly sliced

Combine all ingredients and pour dressing over mixture. Refrigerate mixture for at least 24 hours before serving.

Dressing: 1/4 cup vinegar ·
                   1/4 cup water
                   1 tablespoon liquid artificial sweetener
                   1/2 teaspoon salt
                   1/4 teaspoon pepper

Combine all ingredients and mix well.

FOOD FOR THOUGHT: God is more pleased when we are just and fair than we we give him gifts. Prov. 21:3

DANIEL SALAD

This is excellent for the famous Daniel Fast (God's Answer to Fat — Loose It!) — Thousands have successfully lost tons of fat by this simple ten-day plan. It's good for maintenance of weight also.

45 calories per serving   Serves 6

1 head of lettuce, torn into bite-size pieces
2 ribs of celery, chopped
1/2 head cauliflower, broken apart
1/3 head red cabbage, shredded
1 carrot, shredded
1/3 green pepper, diced
10 fresh mushrooms, chopped
4 radishes, chopped
2 salad onions, chopped
2 tomatoes, chopped

If you don't want to use a salad dressing, cut your lettuce for juice in the salad. A little lemon juice adds zip.

FOOD FOR THOUGHT: God gave Daniel knowledge and skill in all learning and wisdom. Let's ask for it with this salad.

Raw Vegetable Salad Hints:

1. Bean sprouts (easily grown yourself) are a boon to budget and beltline. Not only are they great in salads, but equally good in Chinese dishes and in sandwiches as a change from lettuce.
2. Use spinach in your salad whenever possible — beautiful dark green. Not only does it enhance the appearance of your salad, but spinach is tasty and full of vitamins (more so than iceberg lettuce).
3. Try other kinds of lettuce, whenever available in your market (or grow other kinds) — endive, romaine, Boston Bibb. Put more than one kind in a salad. Add cooked vegetables also to raw vegetables. Try peas, beans, corn or beets.
4. Remember to add your dressings (sparingly) just before serving. Try a variety of garnishes (croutons, sliced hard-cooked eggs, chopped parsley, scallions, sunflower or other seeds) as final touches to give those salads special eye and taste appeal. Be daring, try different dressings!
5. Don't hesitate to add an apple, a few grapes, or some other kind of fruit to your vegetable salads. An apple can really perk up any sad vegetable salad!
6. Try a little of a lot in your combination salads. "Lots" of different ingredients might be tomatoes, radishes, onions, mushrooms, carrots, cucumbers, green peppers, bean sprouts, nuts, or apples. In small quantities they are better than a lot of a few!
7. Try a few spears of asparagus across the top of a tossed salad! A little pimiento adds a lot of color, too!

FOOD FOR THOUGHT: My personal thoughts get into a rut and become bland, but every thought Jesus gives comes directly from heaven where even thoughts never grow old.

SALAD DRESSING SUGGESTIONS

The dressing you put on a salad can make the difference between an "ordinary" salad and a "super" salad, so why be content with less than the best? A salad dressing is limited only by our imagination, just like your Christian life is limited only by your willingness to serve God. Here are some suggestions to add from time to time:

chopped parsley	bacos
green peppers	garlic
horseradish	dill weed
mustard	celery seed
sweetener	chili powder
soy sauce	jalapeno sauce
lemon juice	

Heat your salad dressing occasionally for an entirely different taste.

FOOD FOR THOUGHT: I believe in miracles. I AM ONE!

CREAMED COTTAGE CHEESE DRESSING
120 calories

1/2 cup creamed low-fat cottage cheese
1/4 cup buttermilk
1/2 teaspoon lemon juice
1/8 teaspoon salt

Combine and mix in blender until smooth.

FOOD FOR THOUGHT: Wherever I go, God goes with me, and that makes me a majority!

TOMATO SAUCE

Boil tomato juice down to about 1/2 amount you started with.

Add your choice of spices.

Excellent on salads; but also good as a hot sauce to dip shrimp in, or use over spaghetti; or over eggplant with a little Parmesan cheese.

Can make a barbeque sauce by adding artificial brown sugar and Worcestershire sauce, mustard and onions. Try grilling chicken with this.

FOOD FOR THOUGHT: Lord, what fabulous things are we going to do together today!

COOL CUCUMBER DRESSING

12 calories per serving   Serves 12

1 cup finely chopped cucumbers
1 clove garlic, finely chopped, or garlic powder
1/2 cup chopped green pepper
1/2 teaspoon salt
1/4 cup yogurt
1/4 cup low-calorie mayonnaise
1/4 cup chili sauce
1 tablespoon prepared mustard

This is a real unusual delightful dressing over a wedge of lettuce. For the rest of your family you might add blue cheese if you like.

FOOD FOR THOUGHT: "... each day God added to them all who were being saved." Acts 2:47. Are you saved? If not, ask God to add you to his kingdom right now and ask him to save you — to forgive your sins, and ask Jesus to come into your heart.

COOKED SALAD DRESSING
One calorie per tablespoon

1/2 cup cider vinegar
3 egg yolks
1/2 teaspoon prepared mustard
1/2 teaspoon salt
1/4 teaspoon cayenne pepper or onion powder

In small pan heat vinegar to boiling. In top of double boiler beat egg yolks with seasonings until thick. Pour hot vinegar slowly over. Stir well. Cook in double boiler until thick.

FOOD FOR THOUGHT: ".... forgive us our sins, just as we have forgiven those who have sinned against us." Matthew 6:12

HERBALIZED VINEGAR FOR SALADS
Approximately 886 calories for entire recipe

1 quart cider vinegar
1 teaspoon celery seed
1 teaspoon dill seed
2 cloves garlic
2 tablespoons dark brown sugar
1 teaspoon vegetable salt

Let stand for one week.
Then add 1/3 cup oil (peanut, soya, or corn) to the vinegar. Only small portions are needed for a salad. The calorie count therefore would be minimal.

FOOD FOR THOUGHT: The biggest sin in the world today is ignoring God and compromising with Christianity.

BUTTERMILK DRESSING
3 calories per tablespoon

1 cup buttermilk
1/2 teaspoon onion juice
3/4 teaspoon seasoned salt
1-1/2 tablespoons lemon juice
1/8 teaspoon pepper

1/8 teaspoon oregano
1/8 teaspoon celery
 seed
sprinkle of garlic
 powder

Put all ingredients into blender and blend, or place in jar and shake well. Store in refrigerator until you want to use it and be sure and shake well again before using. This is a real favorite of mine on tossed salads.

FOOD FOR THOUGHT: Don't look at people for what they are, look at their potential!

SPICY DRESSING FOR GREENS
40 calories entire recipe

1/2 cup tomato juice
1 tablespoon grated red onion
1 teaspoon soy sauce
juice of 1/2 lemon
1/2 teaspoon vegetable salt
1/4 teaspoon basil or salad herbs

FOOD FOR THOUGHT: Don't panic . . . . PRAY!

YOGURT DRESSING

Yogurt is a good substitute where a recipe calls for sour cream. Made with partially skimmed milk, 1/2 cup = 60 calories. Combine with diet mayonnaise for a salad dressing. To this you could add one small dill pickle chopped and 1 teaspoon tomato juice for a French or Thousand Island type dressing. Try horseradish, too!

FOOD FOR THOUGHT: "We grow only as we get our nourishment and strength from God." Col. 2:19b

SUPER DIP

325 calories entire recipe

8 oz. creamed low-fat cottage cheese
1 teaspoon lemon juice
1 small can of crab meat or shrimp
 (4-oz. can tiny shrimp figured)

Mix in blender. Instead of potato chips, use melba toast, or pieces of meat, fish, or vegetables.

FOOD FOR THOUGHT: "So we must listen very carefully to the truths we have heard, or we may drift away from them." Hebrews 2:1.

SALAD SUPREME DRESSING

Low low calories

1/4 cup white vinegar
1 tablespoon diet mayonnaise
1 tablespoon Salad Supreme seasoning
1 teaspoon chives
dash of oregano

Mix altogether and pour over your salad.

FOOD FOR THOUGHT: If you're going to pray for rain, take your umbrella with you.

BEVERAGES

Frances serves Charles the milkshake from the cover.

BEVERAGES

SHAKE YOUR OWN FLAVOR!!!

We all need a little pick-up occasionally, especially when calorie watching gets monotonous, or when your food retraining program doesn't seem quite so interesting any more, so here's one of the most fabulous pick-ups I've ever had.

1/3 cup powdered milk   82 calories
1 cup water and ice
1 teaspoon vanilla
5 envelopes Sweet and Low or 5-1/2 grains saccharin

Put in blender and let it go until it gets super thick and creamy. It's unbelievable what happens when you do this.

I also tried it with peppermint flavoring — 4 drops, in addition to the vanilla, and it was one of the most outstanding shakes I've ever had. To be a little more dramatic, put a little red food coloring in the peppermint one, and you might even add a little sprinkling of crushed peppermint stick on the top for interest (interest rate about 5 calories).

Your imagination is the only limit to these — try putting orange flavor in one and then garnish with a slice of fresh orange. Super!! With lemon, garnish with fresh lemon.

If you're real daring, try some almond flavoring, putting a few slivered almonds on the top of the shake. Add a strawberry for color! (See cover picture.)

For another different flavor, sprinkle nutmeg on top of the vanilla milkshake.

More daring — banana flavoring, then nutmeg on top. Put slice of banana on top.

Try apple juice instead of water, and then sprinkle cinnamon on top. Add 40 to 60 calories for the apple juice. (1/2 cup = 60 calories)

Another variation:

12 oz. can of your favorite diet soft drink
1 cup ice cubes
1/4 cup non-fat dry milk
1 teaspoon artificial sweetener

Place everything in blender at high speed until thick. The colder the soft drink, the better the milk shake — try freezing the soft drink first. This could serve two.
Try this with a diet root beer — real great!

FOOD FOR THOUGHT: "Jesus replied that people soon became thirsty again after drinking this water. 'But the water I give them,' he said, 'becomes a perpetual spring within them, watering them forever with eternal life.' " John 4:13-14

SKINNIE STRAWBERRY SHAKE
80 calories per serving   Serves 3

2 cups fresh or frozen unsweetened strawberries
1-1/2 cups skim milk
1 cup ice cubes
2 packages sugar sweetener
dash of cinnamon

Blend at medium speed until smooth and the consistency of ice cream. Super!

FOOD FOR THOUGHT: "Your own soul is nourished when you are kind; it is destroyed when you are cruel." Proverbs 11:17

ORANGE AND EGG PICK-UP

80 calories per serving   Serves 2

1 egg yolk
1 cup fresh unsweetened orange juice
1 glass carbonated water

Mix together in blender. Sprinkle nutmeg on top of each serving. Gets real foamy!

FOOD FOR THOUGHT: Thank you, Jesus, that you're the fastest and best "pick-up" I know of.

PINEAPPLE PLEASURE

80 calories per serving   Serves 4

1/2 cup cold water
6 ice cubes
1/2 cup instant non-fat dry milk
1 tablespoon unsweetened lemon juice
2 tablespoons liquid sweetener or the equivalent

of a sugar substitute in pkg. form
1/4 teaspoon lemon extract
2 drops yellow food coloring
1-1/2 cups unsweetened pineapple juice
Blend altogether until frothy and serve.

Because fresh pineapple is one of my "special" favorites, I keep one around all the time. The center core is hard, but flavorful, and some people don't like to eat it. If you don't, keep that center core refrigerated and serve as a "stirrer" in your Pineapple Shake. Add a strawberry on the top for color.

FOOD FOR THOUGHT: Did you tell God today how much you love him?

PUNCH RECIPES

CRANBERRY-ORANGE FLAVORED PUNCH
52 calories per 8-oz. serving

1 qt. diet iced tea
1 qt. low-calorie cranberry juice
1 qt. orange juice unsweetened
32 oz. ginger ale or similar drink
Makes one gallon delicious low-calorie punch!

FOOD FOR THOUGHT: "Even honey seems tasteless to a man who is full; but if he is hungry, he'll eat anything!" Proverbs 27:7

APPLE PUNCH
69 calories per 8-oz. serving   Serves 6

1/2 teaspoon cinnamon
1/2 teaspoon nutmeg
2 cups unsweetened apple juice
2 cups water
1 cup unsweetened pineapple juice
1 cup unsweetened orange juice
1 teaspoon liquid sweetener
   Blend spices with juices in large bowl or pitcher. Chill well.

FOOD FOR THOUGHT: "Let everything alive give praises to the Lord!" Psalms 150:6

HOLIBERRY PUNCH

10 calories per 5 oz. serving   Serves 38

2 qts. low-calorie cranberry juice
8 teaspoons 100% instant tea dissolved in 2 qts. cold water
2 qts. noncaloric ginger ale
Pour ingredients over ice in punch bowl in order listed.
Dress up with orange slices.

FOOD FOR THOUGHT: "God is so great that we cannot begin to know him. No one can begin to understand eternity." Job 36:26

SPARKLING FRUIT DRINK IDEAS

One can of diet 7-Up, grapefruit, or lemon lime (approximately 2 calories)

Put in blender and add any fruit that appeals to you — fresh strawberries, cantaloupe, raspberries, etc. Turn blender on and you will have a frothy and tart drink that is refreshing. Add calories according to the fruit you use.

FOOD FOR THOUGHT: The Christian life puts sparkle into everyday living!

DESSERTS

COFFEE WHIP

70-75 calories per serving   Serves 6

1 envelope unflavored gelatine
1/2 cup boiling water
2 tablespoons instant coffee
4 envelopes artificial sweetener
1/4 teaspoon almond extract
1 cup non-fat dry milk powder
3/4 cup cold water

Pour boiling water over gelatine, stirring enough to dissolve completely. Add coffee, almond extract and 4 envelopes artificial sweetener. Put in refrigerator until it begins to thicken.

Mix milk powder and cold water and beat until stiff peaks form. Fold into gelatine dessert and then spoon into 6 sherbet dishes. Put back in refrigerator, serve with 1 teaspoon whipped dessert topping.

Super fantastic!

For your family, add whipping cream on top and try some walnuts for a different flavor!

This is a super-pretty one for party gatherings!

FOOD FOR THOUGHT: "Better to live in the desert than with a quarrelsome, complaining woman." Proverbs 21:19

WHIPPED TOPPING

Use cold diet cream soda in place of the milk when preparing. Unusual flavor!

FOOD FOR THOUGHT: Prayer is a hot line to heaven!

STRAWBERRY SURPRISE

Approximately 50 calories each   Serves 2

Here is one of the most fantastic low calorie desserts imaginable.

FOR YOU

2 egg whites, beaten until stiff
1/4 teaspoons cream of tartar
3 envelopes Sweet and Low
2 teaspoons sugar
vanilla flavor to taste

Beat egg whites with 1/4 teaspoons cream of tartar until they really form stiff peaks. Add Sweet and Low, sugar and vanilla. Make two mounds on a cookie sheet sprayed with Pam. Heat oven to 275° and bake for 1 hour. Remove and let sit until cool.

Take fresh strawberries, or fresh pineapple, slice into small pieces. Let sit until juice comes out and then pour over meringue. Delicious! 2 servings — about 50 calories each.

For variation and a real low-calorie dessert, put a little almond flavoring in the meringue and 1 teaspoon Tang. Sprinkle nutmeg on the top and bake for an hour. Super beautiful, delightfully light to eat just as it is. Bakes to a beautiful brown.

FOR THE SKINNIE FAMILY:

One egg white per person and 1/4 teaspoon
  cream of tartar for each two egg whites
1/4 cup sugar for each egg
1/4 cup ground pecans

Beat and put on the same cookie sheet as yours, but make sure you remember which one is yours. You might want to make your family's meringue about 2'' high and bake it as a big pie. Take 1/2 pint whipping cream, beat and spread on top of the meringue. Top with either sugared strawberries, or fruit salad.

This is similar to the Australian dessert, Pavlowa.

You might prefer to do what I do on this dessert. I make it rich for my family, and then eat ONE BITE of it.

FOOD FOR THOUGHT: Does Christianity rub holes in your religion?

PEANUT BUTTER COOKIES
17 calories per cookie   Makes approximately 120 cookies

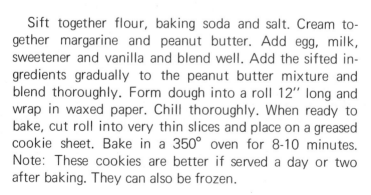

1-1/4 cups all-purpose flour
1/2 teaspoon baking soda
1/2 teaspoon salt
1/2 cup margarine
1/2 cup peanut butter
1 egg, slightly beaten
2 tablespoons milk
4 teaspoons liquid artificial sweetener
1 teaspoon vanilla

Sift together flour, baking soda and salt. Cream together margarine and peanut butter. Add egg, milk, sweetener and vanilla and blend well. Add the sifted ingredients gradually to the peanut butter mixture and blend thoroughly. Form dough into a roll 12" long and wrap in waxed paper. Chill thoroughly. When ready to bake, cut roll into very thin slices and place on a greased cookie sheet. Bake in a 350° oven for 8-10 minutes. Note: These cookies are better if served a day or two after baking. They can also be frozen.

FOOD FOR THOUGHT: Prayer is a two-way street between just you and God.

HAWAIIAN CHEESECAKE

194 calories per serving   Serves 6

CRUST: 4 slices white bread
              5 envelopes artificial sweetener
              1 teaspoon cinnamon
              4 tablespoons shortening

Mix all of this in blender. Pat into pie dish. Bake 400°
10 minutes. Cool.

FILLING: 1 envelope plain gelatin softened in
                1/2 cup lemon-lime diet drink.
              Heat 1 15-ounce can crushed low-calorie
                pineapple.
              Combine with gelatin mixture.
              Chill until set.

COMBINE IN
BLENDER: 1-1/2 cups low-fat cottage cheese
              5 envelopes artificial sweetener
              1 teaspoon vanilla
              pinch of salt
              Add pineapple gelatin mixture to blender
                and blend until smooth.

Pour into chilled crust.

FOOD FOR THOUGHT: A sense of humor is one of God's most
priceless gifts.

HAWAIIAN PINEAPPLE-LIME FLUFF

120 calories per serving   Serves 4

1 package dietary lime gelatin
1-1/2 cups boiling water
1-1/2 cups bottled apple juice (unsweetened)
1 cup canned dietetic pineapple, drained and cut
 into small pieces
1/4 cup milk
1/4 cup grated coconut
1/4 teaspoon vanilla extract
1/2 cup dessert-topping mix

Pour boiling water over gelatin, stirring enough to dissolve completely. Pour in apple juice, then refrigerate until it begins to thicken.

Fold pineapple into gelatin and then put into 6 dessert glasses. Refrigerate until firm.

Combine dessert-topping mix and milk and beat with rotary beater until stiff peaks form. Add coconut and vanilla, and put 1 tablespoon topping on each one. Add strawberry on top for color, or small pieces of pineapple.

A fabulous dessert your entire family will enjoy. For those not concerned with calories, substitute whipping cream for the dessert-topping mix, and add a few nuts!

FOOD FOR THOUGHT: Prayer is just talking to God.

LEMON CHIFFON PIE

64 calories per serving   Serves 6

Crust: 10 graham crackers finely crushed in pyrex dish.
Moisten pan well so crumbs will stick to bottom of dish.
Filling: 4 egg yolks well beaten
               1-1/2 tablespoons powdered artificial
                 sweetener
               1/2 teaspoon salt
               3 tablespoons lemon juice
               1 teaspoon grated lemon rind
               1 tablespoon gelatin
               1/4 cup cold water
               4 egg whites well beaten

In blender put everything but the egg whites, gelatin
and water. Blend thoroughly.
In a cup put the cold water and the gelatin to soften.
Bring to a boil the lemon and egg yolk mixture.
Quickly add the gelatin. Stir well.
Add stiffly beaten egg whites.
Fold egg whites into hot mixture until thoroughly
blended. Pour into crust. Set in refrigerator to chill.

FOOD FOR THOUGHT: More lives are ruined over a cup of coffee
than by the shot of a gun.

STRAWBERRY SHERBET

105 calories per serving   Serves 1

1 cup skim milk
3 large whole strawberries
1/2 envelope artificial sweetener

Mix in blender. Freeze in ice cube tray. When almost
solid, turn out of tray and beat with fork. Refreeze.

FOOD FOR THOUGHT: What you talk about is what you think
about.

TASTE SURPRISE

170 calories entire recipe   Serves 1

1/2 cup large curd, low-fat cottage cheese
1/2 cup unsweetened applesauce
1 tablespoon applebutter

Place cottage cheese in sherbet dish, add applesauce. Top with applebutter. This may be layered more, if you wish. These flavors are very compatible. An alternative to applebutter — grate a bit of nutmeg or use cinnamon.

FOOD FOR THOUGHT: Don't praise yourself; let others do it! Proverbs 27:2

SWEET COOKIE TREAT

195 calories entire recipe   Don't be a pig!

1 ounce raisin bran (1/2 cup)
1 grated apple with skin
1/3 cup milk powder
1 teaspoon vanilla
2 packages sweetener
1/4 teaspoon salt
apple pie spices to taste (optional)

Stir and drop by spoon on non-stick cookie sheet or Pam-sprayed sheet. Bake 325° for 25 minutes. Don't overindulge.

FOOD FOR THOUGHT: What goes into your mind comes out of your mouth.

LOW-FAT ICE CREAM

80 calories per serving (1 cup)   Serves 4

1-1/2 cups fresh peaches
1 egg
1 package dry Carnation milk
2-1/2 cups water
4 envelopes artificial sweetener
1/4 teaspoon flavoring

Blend together and put in freezer tray. When ready to serve, put in blender and mix to consistency of soft ice cream.

FOOD FOR THOUGHT: Learn to put FIRST things FIRST in your life.

CHERRY SURPRISE

Approximately 100 calories per serving   Serves 1

2 ounces low-calorie cherry soda
1/2 cup dry skim milk powder
1 envelope artificial sweetener
6 fresh strawberries

Mix in blender. Add strawberries last. Freeze. Before eating put back in blender until consistency of soft ice cream. Real good!

FOOD FOR THOUGHT: Don't try reading the 29th chapter of Acts, but do try writing your share of this new chapter.

BANANA-APPLE CAKE

106 calories per slice   Serves 12

1/4 cup corn oil
1/2 cup sugar
1 egg white
1 cup flour
1 teaspoon soda
1/4 teaspoon salt
1/2 teaspoon cinnamon
1 cup mashed bananas
1 cup chopped cooking apples
1 teaspoon lemon juice

Spray glass pan
with Pam.
Mix oil, sugar and
egg white.
Add other ingredients.
Bake 350° 25 min.

FOOD FOR THOUGHT: "A worthy wife is her husband's joy and crown; the other kind corrodes his strength and tears down everything he does." Proverbs 12:4

APPLE COOKIES

130 calories for entire recipe   Don't overindulge!

Grate 1 apple, skin and all
Work in 2/3 cup dry milk
2 teaspoons sugar substitute
1/2 teaspoon vanilla

Bake 350° about 10 minutes

CAREFUL !

FOOD FOR THOUGHT: You can't cook your dinner on the stove if you don't turn the stove on.

APPLICIOUS

70 calories per serving   Serves 1

Cut up 1 apple into slices and sprinkle with lemon juice and cinnamon. Eat this way or slip under the broiler for a few seconds. If you broil, you might want to put some artificial sweetener over the top.

FOOD FOR THOUGHT: A "believer" is one who puts into action what he believes.

PINEAPPLE DELIGHT PIE

Approximately 76 calories per serving   Serves 6

2 cups crushed low-calorie pineapple, drained. Put on bottom of pie dish sprayed with Pam.

Boil the following for 2 minutes, cool, and then pour over pineapple.

1 cup water
1 teaspoon vanilla
1 envelope gelatin
1 teaspoon coconut extract
1 teaspoon lemon juice
1/2 teaspoon cinnamon

Topping: 1-1/3 cup powdered dry milk, 2 tablespoons sugar substitute, 1 teaspoon cinnamon. Sprinkle topping on "pie," and bake 350° 30 minutes. Chill.

FOOD FOR THOUGHT: Sharing Jesus is always an adventure.

ORANGE GEL

53 calories per serving   Serves 1

1/4 cup orange juice (unsweetened)
1/4 cup boiling water
1 teaspoon lemon juice
1 teaspoon unflavored gelatin

Mix gelatin, lemon and orange juices together.
After gelatin swells, add boiling water.
Stir well until gelatin dissolves.
Pour into sherbet glass and chill.

FOOD FOR THOUGHT: Sin is the most dangerous of enemies — God is our security.

RICE PUDDING

75 calories per serving   Serves 6

1 qt. skim milk
1 teaspoon liquid artificial sweetener
1/4 cup uncooked rice
1/4 teaspoon nutmeg
1 teaspoon vanilla
1/8 teaspoon salt

Scald milk. Add sweetener and mix well. Add rice, nutmeg, vanilla and salt and stir. Pour into lightly greased baking dish (Pam-sprayed) and bake 300° oven for about 2 hours. Stir several times during first 1-1/2 hours of baking. Cool before serving.

FOOD FOR THOUGHT: Prayer is the answer to loneliness.

PUMPKIN CUSTARD

90 calories per serving   Serves 6

1-1/2 cups canned pumpkin
1-1/2 cups fresh skim milk
2 eggs
2 tablespoons honey
1 teaspoon cinnamon
1/2 teaspoon vanilla
1/2 teaspoon ginger
1/4 teaspoon salt

Combine milk, eggs, honey, vanilla, cinnamon, ginger and salt. Add pumpkin, blend well. Pour into individual 6 ounce custard cups and bake in moderate oven 350° 50-60 minutes or until knife inserted comes out clean.

FOOD FOR THOUGHT: Are you fun to live with?

ORANGE COOKIES

38 calories per cookie   24 cookies

1/4 cup margarine
2 teaspoons liquid artificial sweetener
1/4 cup orange juice
1 tablespoon grated orange peel
1 teaspoon vanilla
1 cup sifted all-purpose flour
1/4 teaspoon baking powder
1/4 teaspoon salt
Optional: 1/2 teaspoon anise seed

Mix all ingredients together well. Drop by teaspoonfuls onto an ungreased cookie sheet. Bake in a 350° oven for about 10 minutes or until tops are lightly browned.

FOOD FOR THOUGHT: The heathen works from sun to sun, but the Christian's work is never done!

COCONUT CHOCOLATE DROPS

34 calories per cookie   Makes 36 cookies

2 eggs
1/2 cup yogurt
1 tablespoon liquid artificial sweetener
1 teaspoon baking soda
1 teaspoon salt
1 square (ounce) unsweetened chocolate, melted
2 tablespoons melted margarine
1 cup sifted flour
2 tablespoons grated coconut

Beat eggs until thick and lemon-colored. Add yogurt, sweetener, baking soda and salt to eggs and mix well. Mix butter and chocolate together and add to egg mixture. Add flour and blend well. Drop by rounded teaspoonfuls onto an ungreased cookie sheet. Sprinkle with coconut. Bake in a 350° oven for 8-10 minutes.

FOOD FOR THOUGHT: Christianity is like anything else — you can't do it halfway and expect it to be all the way.

SUPER BAKED APPLES

41 calories per serving   Serves 3

3 large apples
1 tablespoon frozen orange juice concentrate
2 teaspoons liquid artificial sweetener
cinnamon and nutmeg to taste

Core applies and slice, leaving skins on. Place sliced apples on a large sheet of heavy-duty aluminum foil. Sprinkle with remaining ingredients. Wrap foil tightly and bake in a 350° oven for 20-25 minutes.

FOOD FOR THOUGHT: If you have problems in your marriage, bury them in the sea of forgetfulness.

BANANA CREAM PIE

190 calories per serving   Serves 6

1 baked pie shell
   Fill with 1 large package Instant Vanilla Pudding Mix made with 1-1/2 cups skim milk, and 1 teaspoon vanilla. Beat until thickened.
   Fold in 1-1/2 cups Dream Whip. Arrange slices of two or three bananas in shell. Top with filling. Chill and serve.

   This is super-scrumptious, but high in calories. You might want to cut way back on your dinner just to have a small piece of this fabulous pie!

FOOD FOR THOUGHT: God doesn't ask you to give up something that will do you good.

COCONUT CREAM PIE

140 calories per serving   Serves 6

1 baked pie shell
   Fill with 1 large package Instant Vanilla Pudding Mix made with 1-1/2 cups skim milk.
   Beat until thickened.
   Fold in 1/2 cup coconut. Top with 1-1/2 cups Dream Whip. Chill and Serve

   These pie recipes were all sent in by a friend of mine, and I've tasted them, so I know how delightful they are. I'd rather have a small 1" piece of a super pie, than a half of a pie that wasn't special. Remember this when you make these. Each of these will be fabulous for your family without any additions except to give them a larger piece of pie than Skinnie Minnie needs!

FOOD FOR THOUGHT: Be honest!

SLIM-LINE STRAWBERRIES WITH BUTTERMILK
58 calories per serving   Serves 1

1/2 cup strawberries
1/2 cup of skim buttermilk
1 envelope artificial sweetener

For a real interesting change, make this into ice cream by freezing. Freeze until firm. Break into chunks and beat with an electric mixer until smooth. Freeze firm.

FOOD FOR THOUGHT: Being considerate is one of the most important demonstrations of love.

DELICIOUSLY DIFFERENT ICE
1 calorie per serving   Serves 1

Open your favorite diet soft drink, freeze until solid.

FOOD FOR THOUGHT: Prayer is praising God for what he has done for you.

CANTALOUPE BALLS WITH STRAWBERRIES
55 calories per serving   Serves 6

3 cups cantaloupe balls
2 cups fresh strawberries
3 tablespoons orange or lime juice poured
  over the top.

Chill an hour or more, and then serve.

FOOD FOR THOUGHT: "Don't visit your neighbor too often, or you will outwear your welcome!" Proverbs 25:17

REFRIGERATOR COOKIES

29 calories per cookie   Makes 36 cookies

1-1/2 cups all-purpose flour
1-1/2 teaspoons baking powder
1/4 teaspoon salt
1/4 cup margarine
1/3 cup creamed cottage cheese, low-fat
2 teaspoons liquid artificial sweetener
2 teaspoons vanilla

Sift together flour, baking powder and salt. In large bowl cream together margarine and cottage cheese. Add sweetener and vanilla and beat well. Blend the sifted ingredients gradually into the creamed mixture. Form dough into a roll approximately 9" long. Wrap in waxed paper and chill at least 2 hours. When ready to bake, cut roll into 1/4" slices and place on a greased cookie sheet. Bake in a 350° oven for 12-15 minutes or until tops are lightly browned.

FOOD FOR THOUGHT: I do not understand Christianity, I do not understand electricity, but I don't intend to sit in the dark until I do.

PUMPKIN PIE

133 calories per serving   Serves 6

1 baked pie shell
Fill with 1 large package Instant Vanilla Pudding Mix mixed with 1-1/2 cups pumpkin and 1-1/2 cups skim milk. Beat until thickened. Pour into shell. Add pumpkin pie spices to taste. Top with 1-1/2 cups Dream Whip. Chill and serve.

Another sinful pie, but worth taking away something else, just to have this real taste treat.

FOOD FOR THOUGHT: Don't ask for more faith — act upon what you have.

SWISS "DO-IT-YOURSELF" OATMEAL

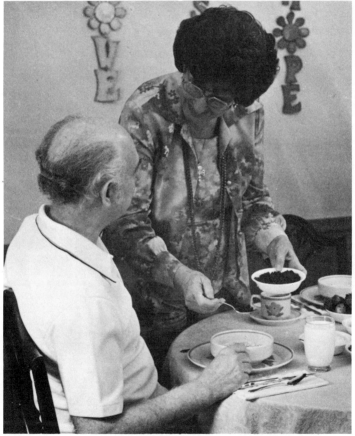

I'm putting raisins in Charles' oatmeal. Note bowls of fresh strawberries, coconut, nuts, fresh pineapple and apples. We are surrounded by Jesus as we eat! (Note signs on wall, LOVE, JESUS, HOPE and JOY.)

A SPECIAL FOR SPECIAL TIMES

SWISS "DO-IT-YOURSELF" OATMEAL

This is one of the most fabulous breakfasts in the world, for your entire family. Each one of them will be able to find something they like to make this delightful dish. This has real "staying" ability, and if you indulge a little yourself, you'll find you can skip the noon meal very easily.

START WITH
Raw, uncooked 3 minute oatmeal   1 oz. = 110 calories

We put bowls of "goodies" on our table when we serve this for company, and into the bowls we put all kinds of things. Some of them are taboo for you, but will add excitement for the rest of your family.   There are plenty for you, too!

FOR YOU
Apples
Pineapple (Fresh)
Pear
Nuts (small amount)
Raisins (very small amount)
Nectarine
Strawberries

Sweetener
Skinnie Minnie Milk
   (low calorie)

FOR YOUR ENTIRE FAMILY
Apples
Pineapple
Pear
Nuts, any amount chopped
Raisins, any amount
Coconut
Dried Apricots

Dates
Nectarine or peach
Strawberries

Sugar
Half and Half

This is a dish that you can add as much, or as little, as you want. We usually put apples, pineapple, nuts and raisins in ours. For variation we add strawberries and Charles uses lots of coconut. Sometimes he'll eat it with just dried apricots, raisins and a sprinkling of nuts.

Add only enough half and half to moisten — don't drown it!

The secret of this dish is making sure that you cut the fruit into very tiny pieces. I do it all on a chopping board and cut the fruit "super small" because the flavor is much more delicate this way. You don't want fruit salad, just a teasing of the fruit! I usually put a teaspoon of apples, pineapple and strawberries in mine, together with a very small amount of nuts and raisins.

The caloric content is WHAT YOU PUT IN IT, so watch out!

This is such a special treat I'm putting it in a section all by itself. It's not exactly a SKINNIE MINNIE recipe, but by watching it, you can enjoy this fantastic breakfast, and make up for any extra calories by forgetting about lunch.

FOOD FOR THOUGHT: "Kind words are like honey — enjoyable and healthful." Proverbs 16:24

LITTLE OL' EGGS

Eggs are a blessing of God!
They are good disguised or plain!
They are a real budget stretcher.
They are fast and easy to cook.
Eggs are high in protein, low in calories!
Eggs can be ALL or part of a meal!
Eggs can be combined with almost any vegetable or meat to make an omelet.

There are only 80 calories in a medium-size egg.

I wondered this week exactly what a "medium-size" egg was because I bought some extra-large ones and they were so small they looked like pullet eggs, but for the most part, I use the above figure as a calorie counter.

Imagination can do wonders with eggs, but even with no imagination an egg is a wonderful creation of God. Eat lots of them.

POACHED EGGS

I have a little egg poacher with a teflon liner which is wonderful because nothing ever sticks to it. I usually moisten it by just wiping a piece of bacon on the surface of the pan. Put the egg in and let it go for 3 minutes. Turns out perfect each time.

FOOD FOR THOUGHT: "God's laws are perfect. They protect us, make us wise, and give us joy and light." Psalms 19:7,8

SCRAMBLED EGGS

Scrambled eggs are one of our favorites, and yet more injustice is done to an egg when scrambled than almost any other way. Here's how we like ours:

1 teaspoon melted butter
  or bacon drippings
4 eggs

1/4 teaspoon salt
pepper to taste
2 tablespoons milk

Heat butter or bacon drippings in small skillet. In separate bowl, break and beat eggs with fork, add milk, salt and pepper. Pour eggs in skillet and cook slowly. As the egg cooks on the bottom, I gently lift up the cooked portion with a big rubber spoon, and keep folding it toward the middle of the pan.

When the eggs are cooked, but moist and shiny, remove them instantly from the pan to the plate. Scrambled eggs are ruined by one or two things. They are cooked too long, or they are left in the skillet too long after they have reached the peak of perfection. Get them out quickly!

Here are some things you can add to your scrambled eggs:

the vegetables left over from your salad sandwich
  (no more than 1/4 cup)
chili powder sprinkled lightly on top
green peppers
onions
mushrooms
bacon crumbles
1 teaspoon finely chopped onion and 1/4 cup grated
  mild Cheddar cheese

parsley
thyme or oregano
tiny pieces of tomato
lemon pepper
sage
tarragon

Every morning will be a delight to your family if you will add something different each time!

You might even want to give it a Mexican flavor and cook the green peppers, onions, mushrooms and tomatoes together for a sauce, then sprinkle with chili powder and pour over scrambled eggs. Ole!

FOOD FOR THOUGHT: Jesus is the only one who can unscramble your life!

FOR THE REST OF YOUR FAMILY

I can't write about eggs without putting in my favorite recipe that I learned when I went to elementary school (a century ago). This was the first thing I ever learned to cook, and we still love it. I don't eat it any more, because it's too heavy on calories, but your family might really enjoy it!

EGGS-A-LA-GOLDENROD

6 hard-cooked eggs   2 cups milk
1 stick butter
1/3 cup flour or cornstarch
2 teaspoons salt
dash black pepper

Melt butter and add flour, salt and pepper. Cook slowly until the mixture bubbles. The secret of a good white sauce is to cook the flour.

Add milk, and stir until smooth. Chop up hard-cooked eggs, and mix gently. Serve on buttered toast. NO, NO for you!

FOOD FOR THOUGHT: Let Jesus live BIG in you!

FLORENTINE EGGS

163 calories per serving   Serves 3

The first time I ate these was in Hawaii, and I enjoyed them so much I ate them for breakfast every day during our stay, so I want to share this recipe with you.

1 package frozen chopped spinach
1 teaspoon salt
1 tablespoon light cream
1 tablespoon butter or margarine
1 teaspoon arrowroot
1/2 cup milk
3 eggs

Cook spinach as the package label directs, and drain well. Add 1/2 teaspoon salt, cream and 1 teaspoon butter. Put into baking dish, making an even layer.

Make white sauce of 2 teaspoons butter, arrowroot and 1/2 teaspoon salt. After this has bubbled and cooked, add milk, and stir until thick.

Break eggs on top of spinach, and pour sauce over entire dish. Bake, uncovered, approximately 15 minutes or until the eggs are whatever doneness you desire and the top is a pretty golden brown.

FOR YOUR FAMILY: Make yours and theirs in separate baking dishes, and add 1/4 cup grated Swiss cheese to theirs.

FOOD FOR THOUGHT: Seven prayerless days makes one weak.

PORTABLE LUNCH IDEAS

Everybody at one time or another in their life, needs to carry a lunch somewhere or other. Maybe you're dashing off to the beauty parlor, or maybe it's just a hectic daily schedule, but when you know one of "those" kind of days is right on you, try fixing a little something the night before that you can eat at the beauty parlor or in the car moments before you go in.

Maybe you're going to a Bible study and know how bad most sandwiches are for the gal who wants to become a Skinnie Minnie .... try toting one of these totable, portable lunches!

CHUNKY EGG SALAD

160 calories per serving. Add additional calories according to what you use.

Cut 2 hard-cooked eggs into chunks. Add celery and mushroom slices to taste. Season with salt and pepper. Add 3/4 teaspoon of finely chopped green onion and a little of the upper greens. Moisten with 1 tablespoon of diet mayonnaise and 1 tablespoon mustard.

For a change in flavor (if you don't have to breathe on anyone), try a little garlic powder and celery seeds.

FOOD FOR THOUGHT: Thank God often for the reason he does a miracle, as well as for the miracle.

CANTALOUPE FILLED WITH FRESH FRUIT
36 calories for cantaloupe; add more for other fruits.

Cut cantaloupe in half (if good-sized). Scoop out seeds. Use melon-ball cutter to scoop out melon and combine with your choice of other fresh fruit (strawberries, blueberries, pineapple . . .) sweeten to taste (if desired) with artificial sweetener and pile into cantaloupe shell. Totes nicely to work in plastic container and will give you a beautiful and satisfying lunch.

FOOD FOR THOUGHT: We can find no freedom except the freedom to give.

POTATO SALAD
Approximately 165 calories entire recipe

Dice 1 medium-size cold boiled potato. Add chopped celery, chopped fresh parsley, minced onion, grated carrot, chopped green pepper . . . Toss gently with diet mayonnaise (approx. 2 tablespoons). Sprinkle with paprika.
For fun, put some Bacos on top!

FOOD FOR THOUGHT: I want to because HE wants me to — that's all!

TROPICAL CHICKEN SALAD
Approximately 185 calories without nuts

Combine 1/2 cup of diced cooked chicken with 4 oz. of crushed pineapple. Add slices of celery and a "tiny" amount of nuts and hold together with just a little diet mayonnaise. (Could use turkey instead of chicken.)
Five cashews = 60 calories! Watch it!

FOOD FOR THOUGHT: If you don't want to hear God, you cannot hear him because of the static you give him.

DILLED CARROT STICKS

8 to 10 tiny young carrots cut lengthwise in quarters. Place in pan and add 1/2 cup of white vinegar, 1/2 cup of water, 1 teaspoon dill weed, salt and pepper.

Cover and simmer until carrots are tender but still crisp.

Refrigerate in liquid several hours or overnight. About 2-1/2 calories per stick!

FOOD FOR THOUGHT: "He gives food to every living thing, for his loving kindness continues forever." Psalms 136:25

ANTIPASTO

50 calories more or less

Combine 1 cup French-style canned green beans with any of the following: sliced celery, pimiento strips, strips of green pepper, radishes, sliced raw mushrooms, raw cauliflowers, carrot strips, diced cucumber. Excellent when you add 1/4 cup of drained canned shrimp. Sprinkle with 2 tablespoons of your favorite dressing (from dressing section of this book). Calories minimal depending upon serving.

For a real surprise, try some raw squash in this!

FOOD FOR THOUGHT: Faith is the diving board from which we spring into action.

SNOW-PEA SALAD

Calorie count will depend upon ingredients used.

Snow-peas are the Chinese pea pods, they come fresh or frozen, and cook in no time at all. For added flavor, cook them in beef or chicken broth.

Cool. Toss a cup of the chilled snow-peas with 3 ounces of roast beef, or white meat chicken or tiny shrimp. (Cut the beef or chicken in julienne strips.) Season with soy sauce instead of salt.

Calories minimal . . . . unless you get "heavy-handed" with the roast beef!

FOOD FOR THOUGHT: Sometimes we get God and ourselves all mixed up — we ask God for what WE want!

MUSHROOM-STUFFED CELERY

Less than 100 calories for entire recipe

Combine 1/2 cup of finely minced fresh mushrooms with the finely chopped white of a hard-cooked egg. Season with seasoned salt mixture and bind together with a little bit of diet mayonnaise. Stuff the grooves of 4 celery stalks. Try this with a tiny cluster of seedless green grapes. It's good for a brownbag lunch.

FOOD FOR THOUGHT: Attitudes can block the truth.

ASPARAGUS SALAD

What could be more tasty than fresh (cooked) asparagus spears and/or canned asparagus thoroughly chilled! Top with seasoned salt and a drizzle of lemon juice. Minimal calories . . .

Use your imagination and add fresh mushrooms and some onion slices! Delightful!

FOOD FOR THOUGHT: The secret of living is giving!

MODEL MENUS

Did you ever wake up and think, "What can I have for breakfast this morning?" Lots of us feel that way.

Often that's followed by, "What can I have for lunch today?" And after that comes, "What can I have for dinner today?"

I've tried to make up a few model menus for you to spark your imagaination, because all meals ought to be interesting to look at and interesting to eat. Remember the lowly baked potato can do wonders for you, and contains exactly the same number of calories as 1/2 corn muffin. Will last you lots longer, too! Try praising God before and after meals. Really helps the indigestion!

Coffee and tea are calorie free. Be sure to add in the cream and sugar if you think you need it!

Apples are a friend to the one who wants to become a Skinnie Minnie. Keep them handy at all times. They are the best hunger-pangs reducer I've ever known. Only 70 calories. If you feel you must go over your limit, add 1/2 apple with lemon juice on top. Slice it in thin wedges for longer eating.

FOOD FOR THOUGHT: Stop right now and put your hands up in the air. Stretch them up as far as you can get them. Look up to heaven. I DARE YOU TO THINK ABOUT ANYTHING BUT GOD WHEN YOU ARE IN THIS POSITION. There's something about lifting "holy hands to God" that does something to all of us. It takes away the things of the world and puts Jesus in the forefront.

The starred items * indicate that actual recipes will be found in the Recipe Section of this book.

BREAKFASTS UNDER 100 CALORIES

1/2 glass (4 oz.) tomato juice	23
1 medium slice whole grain bread toasted	60
	83

1/2 cup fresh strawberries	23
1 slice raisin bread, toasted	65
	88

1/2 cup corn flakes with 1/2 glass milk	95

1 baked potato	90
mushrooms	10
	100

FOOD FOR THOUGHT: Fun is something you TRY to have — joy is a gift from God and Christ Jesus!

BREAKFASTS UNDER 135 CALORIES

1 baked potato (5-1/2 oz.)	90
mushrooms	10
1/2 cup fresh cantaloupe	35
	135

1/2 glass (4 oz.) prune juice	40
1/2 English muffin toasted	70
with 1/2 teaspoon margarine	17
	127

1/2 cup 100% bran flakes with	
1/2 cup skim milk	97
1 plum, fresh	25
	122

1 nectarine	30
1 pancake	60
1/2 teaspoon butter, melted	17
lemon juice	3
1/2 teaspoon sugar	20
	135

Lemon-butter pancakes are a real delicacy.

FOOD FOR THOUGHT: "Then Abraham ran back to the tent and said to Sarah, 'Quick! Mix up some pancakes! Use your best flour.' " Genesis 18:6

BREAKFASTS UNDER 150 CALORIES

1/2 cup diced fresh cantaloupe	35
1 egg cooked the way you like it	
(except not scrambled)	80
1 slice Zwieback toast	31
	146

1/2 glass (4 oz.) orange juice, unsweetened	60
1 slice rye bread, toasted	60
	120

baked potato	90
with 1/4 cup mushrooms	20
1/2 glass (4 oz.) tomato juice	23
	133

FOOD FOR THOUGHT: Be stubborn only in your relentless desire to serve our Lord Jesus Christ!

BREAKFASTS UNDER 200 CALORIES

1/2 glass (4 oz.) unsweetened grapefruit juice	40
1 egg scrambled with tablespoon milk, teaspoon butter	125
	165

1/2 grapefruit	60
1 egg, boiled	80
1 strip bacon	45
	185

1 medium banana sliced	100
1/2 corn muffin	90
	190

FOOD FOR THOUGHT: If you can find a truly good wife, she is worth more than precious gems! . . . She gets up . . . to prepare breakfast for her household . . . Prov. 31:10, 15

BREAKFASTS UNDER 250 CALORIES

1/2 glass orange juice	60
1 slice whole-wheat toast	60
with 1/8 teaspoon margarine	4
1 poached egg	80
1 strip bacon	45
	249

1/2 cup fresh raspberries	35
over 1 cup corn flakes	100
with 1 teaspoon sugar	20
and 1 cup skim milk	90
	245

1/2 cup blueberries	40
with 1 teaspoon sugar	20
and 1 tablespoon 1/2+1/2 cream	20
1 egg, scrambled	80
with 1/2 teaspoon margarine	17
with 1/2 cup mushrooms, onions &	
green pepper	20
1 slice toast	35
	232

2 fresh apricots	37
3 oz. drained salmon	120
with lemon juice	05
1 thin slice toast	35
with 1/2 teaspoon butter	17
	214

1/2 cup apple juice	60
2 pancakes	120
1/2 teaspoon butter	17
2 teaspoons diet strawberry preserves	8
1 strip bacon	45
	250

FOOD FOR THOUGHT: "God's laws are perfect . . . . They are sweeter than honey dripping from a honeycomb." Psalms 19:7-10

LUNCHES UNDER 175 CALORIES

Vanilla Shake*	82
Wilted Lettuce Salad*	60
2 wheat thins	18
	160

Reuben Sandwich*	175
coffee black or tea	

pizza*   165
coffee black or tea

Leaf Lettuce Chicken Sandwich*   115
8 oz. Cranberry Orange
  Flavored Punch   52
                                               167

Orange & Egg Pick-Up*   31
Filet of Flounder in Foil*   100
Cantaloupe Balls with Strawberries*   44
                                               175

Skinnie Strawberry Shake*   72
Chunky Egg Salad*   100
                                               172

Antipasto*   50
Pineapple Pleasure*   80
2 Peanut Butter Cookies*   34
                                               164

2 Sesame Wafers*   48
Sauerkraut Salad*   29
Low-Fat Ice Cream*   80
                                               157

1/4 head lettuce   15
1 3 oz. can shrimp   100
  with soy sauce   3
decorate with slices of
green pepper, fresh mushrooms   5
4 spears asparagus   10
reducer's dressing   10
3 triangle thins   24
                                               167

FOOD FOR THOUGHT: Let us break bread together, in harmony; in unity, in peace, in love, in patience, in giving to one another. Just as we can make God happy by doing everything to please him instead of ourselves, so we can make our family members happy by doing everything we can to please them.

LUNCHES UNDER 225 CALORIES

3 oz. lean ground beef broiled	140
1/2 cup coleslaw	60
1/2 cup fresh strawberries	23
	223

3 oz. chicken breast	115
4 asparagus spears	10
1 glass skim milk	90
	215

if you are not a milk drinker	
have a fresh pear or banana	100
or some other fresh fruit	

3 heaping tablespoons tuna salad	185
1/2 slice whole-wheat bread	30
	215

1/2 cup V-8 juice	21
1/2 cup cottage cheese creamed	130
1/2 cup diced cantaloupe	36
	187

1 cup Navy bean soup	170
2 saltines	25
1/2 cup grapes	30
	225

LUNCHES UNDER 275 CALORIES

carrot and raisin salad,	
3 heaping teaspoons	150
1/2 English muffin toasted	70
1 med. fresh peach	35
	255

1 oz. melted cheese on	
1 slice whole-wheat bread	165
1/2 tomato sliced	20
1 glass skim milk	90
	275

substitute fruit for milk if you are not
a milk drinker

FOOD FOR THOUGHT: "What dainty morsels rumors are. They are eaten with great relish!" Proverbs 18:8

LUNCHES UNDER 325 CALORIES

3 heaping tablespoons chicken and	
celery salad	185
1 slice whole-wheat bread	60
1 cup fresh raspberries	70
	315

3/4 cup tossed salad, mixed	
vegetables with	30
1 tablespoon thousand island dressing	80
1 all meat frankfurter	170
2 med. fresh apricots	37
	317

DINNERS UNDER 350 CALORIES

3 oz. chicken breast baked	115
1/2 cup mushrooms	10
with 1 teaspoon margarine	34
1 cup asparagus	30
1 sliced tomato	40
1 cup raw diced pineapple	75
	304

1 serving Salmon Casserole*	245
1 serving Yogurt Cucumber Salad*	100
	350

1 serving Beef & Rice	
Stuffed Peppers*	130
1 serving Mixed Vegetable Salad*	105
1 serving Pineapple Delight Pie*	55
	290

1/4 head lettuce	15
6 slices cucumber	5
1/2 tomato sliced	20
1/2 stalk celery	2
1/2 cup raw cauliflower	12
with 1 tablespoon French diet dressing	0
2 oz. boiled ham, sliced	135
1 med. slice cheese	105
1 plum fresh	25
	319

FOOD FOR THOUGHT: "A dry crust eaten in peace is better than steak every day along with argument and strife." Proverbs 17:1

Bean Sprout, Cheese, and Mushroom Toast Treat*	200
Cantaloupe Filled With Fresh Fruit*	60
2 refrigerator cookies*	58
	318

1 serving Fresh Spinach Soup*	75
1 serving Slim Living Shepherd Pie*	130
1 slice Banana-Apple Cake*	90
	295

FOOD FOR THOUGHT: He Lives!

DINNERS UNDER 375 CALORIES

3 oz. veal cutlet, broiled	185
1 baked potato (medium)	90
with 1/4 cup mushrooms	20
1/2 cup cooked green beans	15
1 baked apple (small)	65
	375

EAT THE CANDLE ONLY

4 oz. shrimp, broiled	104
tossed salad, mixed vegetable 3/4 cup with lemon & vinegar dressing (1 tablespoon)	35
1 baked potato	90
with 1/2 teaspoon butter	17
1/2 cup diced fresh pineapple	33
and 1/2 banana	50
and 1/2 orange segments	32
	361

FOOD FOR THOUGHT: "The good man eats to live, while the evil man lives to eat." Proverbs 13:25

DINNERS UNDER 500 CALORIES

1 5 oz. potato baked	85
1 bouillon cube	7
1/2 onion (1/2 cup)	21
with seasoning salt	
3 oz. lean beef broil	140
1 cup green beans	30
1 serving Daniel Salad*	45
	328

1 serving Creamed Cauliflower Soup*	18
1 Veal Scaloppine with Lemon*	210
1 serving Three-Way Salad*	81
1 baked potato	85
with 1/2 teaspoon butter	17
	411

1/2 cup coleslaw*	60
1 serving Meat Loaf Burgers*	300
1 serving Baked Acorn Squash*	107
1 Gelatin Dessert*	14
	481

1 serving Italian Gazpacho*	36
1 serving Sweet and Sour Meatballs*	200
2/3 cup Minute Rice	124
1 serving Cherry Surprise*	100
	460

1 serving Spinach Soufflé *	115
1 Grilled Lamb Chop*	130
1 Lime-Pineapple Salad*	60
1 serving Coconut Cream Pie*	140
	445

IS IT WORTH IT?

THIS

OR THIS
YES!!!

CALORIE CHART

All bran cereal	1/2 cup	92
Almonds, salted	10 to 12 nuts	95
Angel-food cake	1 piece (1/10 of an average cake)	145
Apple	1 medium	70
Apple juice	1/2 cup	60
Applesauce, no sugar	1/2 cup	50
Apricot juice	1/2 cup	60
Apricots, dried	4 to 6 halves, raw	80
Apricots, fresh	2 medium	37
Artichoke, French	1 medium	45
Asparagus, fresh, canned, or frozen	4 medium stalks, drained	10
Avocado	1/4 medium	90
Bacon, fried	1 strip	45
Banana, fresh	1 medium	100
Bean sprouts, canned	1/2 cup	10
Bean sprouts, raw (soy)	1/2 cup	16
Beans, kidney	1/2 cup, cooked	125
Bean, snap; fresh, canned, or frozen	1 cup, drained	30
Beef consomme	1 cup	34
Beef, rib roast	4-1/2"x3"x1/2" slice	265
Beef, lean ground	3 oz.	185
Beef, lean roast	3 oz.	125
Beef soup, noodle	1 can, condensed	155
Beef steak, sirloin, fat trimmed	3 oz.	220
Beef, vegetable, barley soup	1 cup	74
Beets, canned	1 cup, diced, drained	55
Blackberries, fresh	1 cup	60
Blueberries, canned	1/2 cup, with syrup	125
Blueberries, fresh	1/2 cup	45
Blueberries, frozen	1/2 cup, with sugar	90
Bluefish, baked with 1 teaspoon butter	3 oz.	135

Bologna	4-1/2"x1/8" slice	65
Bouillon	1 cup	25
Bouillon cube	1	5–7
Bran, dry cereal	1/2 cup	75
Bran flakes	1 cup	120
Bran muffin	1 med	105
Bran, raisin	1 cup	150
Brazil nuts	2 med	60
Broccoli	1/2 cup drained	20
Broccoli	1 stalk	45
Brussels sprouts	1 cup	55
Butter	1 tablespoon	100
Buttermilk	1/2 pt	85
Cabbage	1 cup, cooked	30
Cabbage	1 cup, shredded, raw	20
Cantaloupe or muskmelon	1/2 cup diced	20
Carrot & raisin salad	3 teaspoons, heaping	150
Carrots, canned, cooked	1 cup	30
Carrot, raw	1, 5-1/2"x1"	20
Carrot, raw	1 cup diced or shredded	45
Cashew nuts	8 med	90
Catsup	1 tablespoon	15
Cauliflower	1 cup, raw	25
Cauliflower	1 cup, cooked	30
Celery	1 stalk or heart, 8x1-1/2 inch	5
Celery	1 cup diced	15
Celery soup, cream of	1 can, condensed	215
Cereal, Special K	1 cup	70
Chard, Swiss	1/2 cup leaves and stalks, cooked	15
Cheddar cheese, natural	1 oz, 1 inch cube	115
Cheese, American	1 slice, 1 oz.	105
Cherries, fresh, sweet	20 to 25 small	60
Chicken breast, baked	3 oz., skin removed	115
Chicken consomme	1 cup	23
Chicken-gumbo soup	1 cup	58
Chicken livers	3 oz.	140
Chicken, roasted	3 slices, 3-1/2"x2-1/2"x1/4"	200

Chicken & celery salad	3 tablespoons heaping	185
Chicken, stewed	1/2 breast or 1 thigh	200
Chicory or endive, curly	10 small inner leaves	5
Chives, raw	1 tablespoon chopped	3
Chop suey	1 cup, chicken, pork	350-400
Clams, raw, shelled, fresh	3 oz.	65
Coconut, dried	2 tablespoons, shredded	85
Coconut, fresh	1"x1"x1/2" piece	55
Coconut, moist	2 tablespoons, shredded	50
Coffee, black	—————	——
Cola beverages	1 bottle, 6 oz.	80
Coleslaw	1/2 cup	60
Collards, cooked	1 cup	76
Consomme	1 can, condensed	101
Corn, canned	1 cup, drained	170
Corn, cream-style, canned	1/2 cup	85
Corn, fresh	1 med. ear (5x1-3/4 in.)	70
Cornmuffin	1/2 muffin	90
Corned beef, canned	3"x2-1/4"x1/4" slice	70
Cornflakes	1 cup	100
Cottage cheese, low-fat	1 cup	193
Cottage cheese, dry	1 rounded tablespoon	30
Crab, canned	3 oz.	85
Crab, deviled	1 med. crab	185
Cracked-wheat bread	1 av. slice	60
Cracker, triangle, thin	2	24
Cracker, wheat thin	2	18
Cracker, salted	2-2" sq.	25
Cracker, soda	2-1/2" sq.	25
Cranberry juice	1/2 cup	80
Cream, heavy	1 tablespoon	50
Cream, light	1 tablespoon	30
Cream-of-wheat	1 cup, cooked	130
Creamed soups, various	1 cup (varies)	135
Cucumber	1/2 med., or 6 slices	5

Edam cheese	1 oz.	85
Egg, boiled	1 med.	80
Egg, fried	1 med., 1 teaspoon fat	110
Egg, poached	1 med.	80
Egg, white only	1 large	17
Egg, raw, whole	1 med.	80
Egg, yolk only	1 large	59
Egg, scrambled	1 med., 1 tablespoon milk, 1 teaspoon diet margarine	100
Eggplant	3 slices, 4" diam. or 1 cup diced	50
Endive, Belgian	10 long leaves; 15 to 20 small leaves	10
English muffin	1/2 muffin	70
Escarole	2 large leaves	10
Figs, fresh	3 small, 1-1/2 diam.	90
Flounder, baked filets	3 oz.	126
Frankfurter, pure beef	1 each	136
French dressing, commercial	1 tablespoon	65
Fruit cocktail, canned	6 tablespoons fruit and juice	70
Gelatin dessert	1/2 cup, any flavor	80
Gelatine salad with fruit	2-1/2" sq., or 1 cup	170
Gelatine, salad with vegetables	2-1/2" sq.	115
Gelatine, unflavored	1 tablespoon	35
Ginger ale	1 glass, 6 oz.	60
Gingersnap	1 small	15
Graham cracker	2 small, 2-1/2" sq.	55
Grape juice	1/2 cup	80
Grapefruit, fresh	1/2 medium	50
Grapefruit juice, canned, sweetened	1/2 cup scant	65
Grapefruit juice, canned, unsweetened	1/2 cup scant	50
Grapefruit juice, fresh	1/2 cup	45

Grapes, American	22 to 24, or 1 cup	65
Grapes, Malaga or Tokay	22 grapes	100
Grapes, seedless white	60 grapes	100
Griddlecake, buckwheat	4" diam	50
Griddlecake, white	4" diam	60
Ham, boiled	4"x2-1'2"x1/8" slice	90
Ham, smoked, lean, baked	3 oz. fat trimmed	245
Hash, beef	1 cup	290
Hominy or grits	1/2 cup, cooked	120
Honeydew melon	1 slice, 2" x 7"	50
Kale	1 cup	45
Lamb chop, rib, broiled	1 chop	130
Lamb chop, loin, broiled	1 chop, 2.6 oz. fat trimmed	140
Lemon, fresh	1 medium	20
Lemon, juice	1 tablespoon	4
Lettuce	1 head about 4"	30
Lime, fresh	1 medium	20
Liver, beef	2 oz	130
Lobster, fresh, boiled or broiled	4 oz	108
Luncheon meat	4"x8-1/2"x1/9" slice	80
Margarine, diet	1 tablespoon	50
Mayonnaise, commercial	1 tablespoon	65
Melba toast	2 slices, rounds	16
Milk, skim	1 cup	90
Milk, whole	1 cup	160
Milk, dry, non-fat	1 tablespoon	20
Milk, dry, non-fat	1 cup	82
Mushrooms, canned	1-4 oz. can, drained	15
Mushrooms, fresh	1 cup sliced	20
Navy bean soup	1 cup	170
Nectarines	1 medium	30
Noodles	1 cup, cooked	105
Nuts, mixed	8 to 12	95

Oatmeal, cooked	1 cup	150
Oatmeal, uncooked	1/4 cup	83
Oil and vinegar	1 tablespoon	65
Okra	8 pods	30
Onions, raw, sliced	1/2 cup	21
Onion, raw	1 large	40
Onions, green (scallions)	6 small	20
Orange	1 medium	65
Orange-and-grapefruit juice, canned, sweetened	1/2 cup	65
Orange-and-grapefruit juice, canned, unsweetened	1/2 cup	50
Orange juice, canned, sweetened	1/2 cup	70
Orange juice, fresh	1/2 cup	50
Orange juice, frozen	1/2 cup, reconstituted	50
Parmesan cheese, dry, grated	1 tablespoon	25
Parsley	10 sprigs	5
Parsnips, cooked	1 cup	95
Peaches, dried, cooked	3 halves, 2 tablespoons juice	125
Peach, fresh	1 medium	35
Peaches, frozen	1/2 cup	90
Pear, fresh	1 medium average	90
Peas, canned	1 cup, drained	165
Peas, fresh or frozen	1 cup, cooked	140
Pecans	12 halves	105
Pepper, green or red	1/2 cup diced	10
Pickle, dill or sour	1 large	15
Pickles, mixed sweet	4 small pieces	25
Pickle, sweet	1 small	20
Pimiento, canned	1 medium	10
Pineapple, chunks, canned	1/2 cup, with juice	95
Pineapple, chunks, frozen	1/2 cup, with juice	95
Pineapple, crushed, canned	1/2 cup, with juice	100
Pineapple, fresh, with sugar	1/2 cup, diced	75

Pineapple, fresh, without sugar	1/2 cup, diced	35
Pineapple, juice	1/2 cup	60
Pineapple, sliced, canned	3/4" thick slice, 2 tablespoons juice	95
Plums, canned	3 med., 2 tablespoons juice	90
Plum, fresh	average	25
Popped corn	1 cup, no fat	55
Postum	1 cup	35
Potato salad	1/2 cup	185
Potatoes, scalloped	1/2 cup	130
Potato, white, baked, no butter or margarine	1 medium	90
Potato, sweet, baked	1 medium	155
Potatoes, white, creamed	1/2 cup	115
Potatoes, white, mashed	1/2 cup, scant	125
Prune juice	1/2 cup	85
Prunes	4 to 5 med., 2 tablespoons juice	120
Puffed rice	1 cup	55
Puffed wheat	1 cup	45
Pumpkin pie	1 cup	75
Radish	4 small	7
Raisin bread	1 slice, av.	65
Raisins	1/4 cup	110
Raspberries, canned	1/2 cup, 2 tablespoons juice	100
Raspberries, fresh, red	1/2 cup	35
Raspberries, frozen	1/2 cup	85
Rhubarb, stewed	1/2 cup, sweetened	140
Rice, converted	1/2 cup, cooked	100
Rice, wild	1/2 cup, cooked	90
Rolled oats	1/2 cup, cooked	75
Romaine	1 large leaf	2
Roquefort cheese, salad dressing	1 tablespoon	76
Russian dressing	1 tablespoon	74
Rutabaga	1/2 cup	25
Rye bread, light	1 slice, thin	60
Rye wafer	1 double square wafer	20

Salad dressing	1 tablespoons cooked type	60
Salad oil	1 cup	1,945
Salmon, fresh or frozen	3 oz.	85
Salmon, boiled	4"x3"x1/2" piece	170
Salmon, canned	1/2 cup	100
Sardine	3 oz., drained	175
Sauerkraut, canned	1/2 cup, drained	15
Sherbet	1 cup	235
Shad, fresh, baked	3 oz.	127
Shredded wheat	1 biscuit	100
Shrimp, fresh or frozen	4 oz.	104
Shrimp, canned	4 oz.	132
Soda water, plain	—————	————
Sour cream	1 tablespoon	30
Soy sauce	1 oz. (2 tablespoons)	19
Spaghetti, canned	3/4 cup	100
Spaghetti, cooked, plain	1 cup	110
Spinach, canned or cooked	1 cup	40
Spinach, fresh	1/2 cup	14
Spinach, raw	1/2 pound	50
Squash, summer, yellow	1 cup, cooked	30
Squash, winter	1 cup, cooked	130
Strawberries, fresh	1/2 cup	27
Strawberries, frozen	1/2 cup	90
Sugar, brown, light or dark	1 tablespoon	50
Sugar, confectioners'	1 tablespoon	40
Sugar, white, granulated	1 tablespoon	50
Sweet potato, baked	1 medium	185
Swordfish, fresh or frozen	3 oz.	150
Swiss cheese	1 oz.	100
Tangerine	1 medium	40
Tapioca pudding	1/2 cup	135
Tartar sauce	1 rounded tablespoon	95
Tea, plain	—————	————
Thousand Island Dressing	1 tablespoon	120
Tomato juice	1/2 cup	25
Tomato paste	1 tablespoon	10
Tomato puree	1 tablespoon	5

Tomato sauce, canned	1/2 cup	85
Tomatoes, canned	1 cup	50
Tomato, fresh, raw	1 medium	40
Tuna, water packed, drained	4 oz	144
Turkey, cooked, skin removed	3 oz	151
Turnip greens	1/2 cup, cooked	25
Turnips, white	1/2 cup cubes, cooked	25
Vegetable-juice cocktail	1/2 cup	20
Vegetable salad, tossed	3/4 cup, without dressing	30
Vegetable soup, homemade	3/4 cup	95
Waldorf salad	3 tablespoons, heaping	150
Walnuts, English	8 to 12 halves	100
Watercress	10 sprigs	2
Watermelon	4 x 8 wedge	120
Watermelon	1 cup cubes & balls	55
Wheat cereal, dry (Wheaties)	1 cup	110
White bread, enriched	1 slice, av.	60
White bread	1 extra thin (5/16") slice	45
White sauce, medium	1/4 cup	105
Whitefish, fried	3"x3"x1" piece	185
Whole-wheat, wafer	2" sq.	25
Worcestershire sauce	1 tablespoon	11
Yogurt, low-fat	1 cup	125
Zwieback	1 piece	31
Zucchini	1/2 cup, cooked	23

NOTES

NOTES

NOTES